Diana Farr Louis

ATHENS
and beyond:
30 Day Trips & Weekends

ATHENS NEWS

ISBN 960-86395-3-0

© Diana Farr Louis,
Athinaika Nea S.A., 2003

Published by Athens News
3, Christou Lada Str.
Athens 102 37
www.athensnews.gr

Old stone bridge in Tinos

ATHENS  NEWS

The chapters of this book were originally published, over a period of seven years, in the Athens News. They have since been updated and enriched with new information.

The Athens News is Greece's historic, English-language newspaper. Founded ini 1952 by Yannis Horn, it has been part of the Lambrakis group of publications since 1993. In 2001 the newspaper ceased its daily publication and became a weekly. It is distributed throughout Greece and to selected sales points abroad.

Andros town

*For my beloved sister Nancy
who would have been so pleased.*

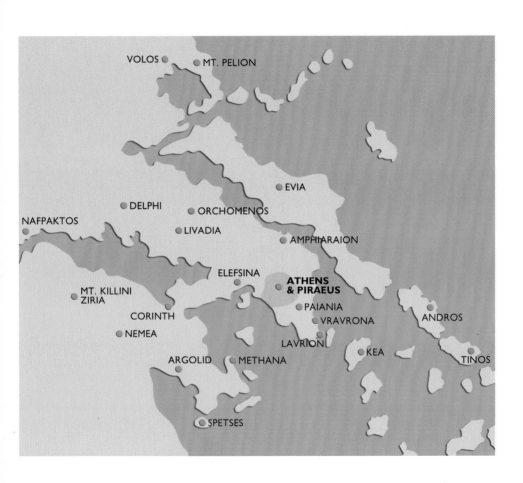

VOLOS • MT. PELION

EVIA

DELPHI • • ORCHOMENOS

NAFPAKTOS • LIVADIA

AMPHIARAION

ELEFSINA • **ATHENS & PIRAEUS**

MT. KILLINI ZIRIA

PAIANIA

CORINTH

VRAVRONA

ANDROS

NEMEA

LAVRION

ARGOLID • METHANA

KEA

TINOS

SPETSES

Table of Contents

INTRODUCTION

I first came to Greece in the summer of 1963. Fresh out of college, I picked up a new VW beetle in Paris and drove through France, Northern Italy and Yugoslavia with my younger brother. We didn't pay much attention to Dijon, Venice or Dubrovnik, so intent were we on getting to Greece, the 'in' country among students in the early 60s. We had heard so much about the hospitality, the 'kefi' (although we didn't know the Greek word for *joie de vivre* yet), the antiquities and, of course, the romantic islands.

I remember crossing into Greece at Evzoni and feeling my spirits lift. Yugoslavia had felt repressed and alien to us Americans, but the peasants riding home in colorful horse-driven carts waved so warmly, with such broad smiles, that we knew Greece would be different.

And it was. After a few days in Athens, we headed straight for Spetses, where a college friend who was half-Greek had told me she'd be all summer. We had no other contacts, but as it turned out we didn't need any. In those days private houses on islands rarely had phones, so we decided to sit in a café in the port until she showed up. In the meantime, we made new friends – some who are still among my closest – and by the time Marinette appeared, my brother had decided Spetses was all he'd ever need to know of Greece. There were beautiful people, beaches, open-air discos, picnics, boat rides, buggy rides, conversations under falling stars… who cared about the lack of ruins?

Determined to see more of the country, I dragged him to Mykonos, the Acropolis on a moonlit night and a play at Epidavros. In mid August, after he'd left for the States, I visited Crete, Delphi, Meteora, Metsovo, Yiannina and Corfu. By the end of the summer I was in love; not with just one Greek, but with the Aegean and the mountains, jasmine-scented evenings, figs picked at sunrise and lots and lots of people. Were my sun-glasses rose tinted, was I just lucky or were things different back then? Everyone I seemed to meet, whether young and privileged or simple and homespun, shepherd or shipowner, was kind, intelligent, warm and filled with an ability to enjoy life to a degree I'd never encountered before.

That winter in Paris I played Theodorakis and Hadjidakis more than Piaf and Françoise Hardy and ate *dolmadakia* at a little Greek taverna on the Rive Gauche. My favorite book was an album called *La Grèce que j'aime*.

A year later, I returned to Spetses, at the end of October, during a succession of days called 'hara Theou' or joy of God. Not a cloud in the sky, swims in effervescent waters, bougainvillea tumbling over white walls, and, this time, a man, a Greek to love. We married in New York and I spent every summer in Greece, sometimes an Easter or a New Year's, for the next five years. In 1970 we split up, and by 1972, after a year in Italy, I was back, living in Maroussi with my six-year-old son, Petros.

I started writing almost as soon as I moved here – though not for publication – about the absurdities of Greek life. I also started exploring. Petros and I went all over the Peloponnese in our tiny *cinquecento*, scrambling up and down Crusader castles, discovering trilobites in the columns of the temples at Olympia and picnicking in fields of flamingo-pink gladioli. We searched for the mysterious Isle of Gla in the drained lake of Kopaida, watched boys leap over bonfires on Midsummer's Eve in Andros, and slept on the sand on Serifos. Whenever I could, I went sailing with friends: in the Ionian, Cyclades, Dodecanese and Sporades. We anchored in solitary coves, gorged on mountains of sea urchins, shivered under our oilskins in a 9 Beaufort meltemi, and sweltered in the open Aegean, windless and miles from anywhere. But the mountains lured me too. Iti and Ohi, Parnassos and Pendeli, Taygetos, Ghiona, Helmos, the Vikos Gorge…

I was insatiable. Greece was a sumptuous buffet table and I wanted to taste every single delicacy. Eventually, exploring Greece became more than a hobby; it became a job and I actually earned money (never very much of course) travelling around the country. First I was commissioned to write a guidebook to the Ionian, then I was asked to contribute chapters on certain regions in more comprehensive books – the *Penguin, Berlitz and Fodor's* guides to Greece. This in turn led, by a more devious route, to the writing of two cookbooks, *Prospero's Kitchen, Mediterranean Cooking of the Ionian Islands from Corfu to Kythera* (1995), and *Feasting and Fasting in Crete* (2001).

In the meantime, in March of 1997, Romolo Gandolfo, then editor of the *Athens News*, asked if I'd like to write travel pieces for the paper. "We need someone who can write about places without going there," he said. That idea was to me anathema, and I have never had to resort to it, though I have on occasion sifted through memories to make a story richer. But I was lucky that first year because my new assignment coincided with trips to Crete to research the second cookbook and being hired by the *Rough Guide* to update their material on Central Greece and the Sporades.

Since then I've written pieces on places as farflung as Kastellorizo and Didymoteicho, Paxi and Koroni, and even about trips abroad to New Orleans, Amsterdam, Provence, the Turkish coast and Italy, but over the years I've made a point of writing about places closer to home, archaeological sites and beautiful spots that readers in the Athens area could get to easily. Magical though they may be, I have purposely avoided the major sites, such as Delphi, Nafplion and Mycenae, for example, and tried instead to highlight lesser known locations a reader might have overlooked. It is these articles you'll find collected here. We have grouped them into three sections: Athens and Attica, the Peloponnese and Central Greece and nearby islands. These articles written between 1997 and 2003 (and updated for this edition), were never intended to take the place of a guidebook; instead they are aimed at giving you ideas on where to go on a Sunday morning, a day trip or a short weekend.

This being Greece, many of the articles take archaeological sites as a starting point. By retelling (a judicious amount of) history and myth, seasoned with reminiscences and personal impressions, I try to convey to you what about it fascinates me.

I feel so privileged to have Greece as my second home. Is there any other country of this size that is so varied in its landscape, so complex in its culture, so full of echoes that give its stunning scenery extra resonance? I think of finding grafitti scratched by athletes as they waited in the tunnel to the Nemea stadium or straddling granite columns left high on Mt. Ohi by the Romans. Virtually everywhere you go there are layers and layers of civilization, and with each one you peel off comes a sense of the people who made them: who worshipped at the temples and who laid the masonry, who painted the frescoes and who camped inside the fortresses, who fought at Marathon, at Dervenakia and at Thebes.

And as an added fillip to the wonders of the past you are never far from the singular pleasures of modern Greece: wild flowers, beaches, views, and above all tavernas, their often eccentric owners and the occasional gregarious customer. Is there a better way to savor what you've just experienced than discussing it over a platter of lambchops or *barbounakia*, an array of delicious *mezedakia* and a kilo of local wine?

That said, Greece has changed a great deal in the last forty years. I have seen paved roads replace goat paths, pristine shores turn into booming resorts, television reduce a boisterous *kafeneio*n to near silence and fires blacken whole mountains in a few hours, but I've also watched cozy, comfortable hotels go up in isolated mountain villages and splendid new museums open near forgotten sites. Too much tourism in some places has made many locals suspicious of strangers and prone to rudeness. Nevertheless, one smile can usually coax another, a few words of Greek can unleash a torrent of questions, and if you are open and appreciative, you will probably find the Greeks you encounter on your excursions kind and helpful. *Ta panta rei* – 'All is flux' – as Heraclitus observed. But the things I loved about Greece when I first came here are still with us. We just have to search a little harder.

30
Day
Trips
Athens and Attica
&
Weekends

A river runs through it:
Athens' ancient graveyard

Why is it that of my first visit to the Kerameikos, the ancient cemetery of Athens at the bottom of Ermou Street, my most vivid memory concerns hopping frogs? Our guide must have been telling the group fascinating details about the site, pointing out landmarks and bringing the place of the dead back to life, but her commentary has left no trace in my mind. Instead, it has been supplanted by a vision of totally unexpected yellow-and-green spotted creatures croaking by the side of a stream.

The Eridanos River makes Kerameikos more than just an interesting collection of tombs and historic walls.

I suppose it is a measure of how thirsty we Athenians are for nature that the presence of any wildlife other than pigeons, alleycats and mangy dogs can be more exciting than a historic monument. For Athens holds the dubious honor of having the lowest ratio of green to cement of any major European city. And while Paris, Rome, London, Prague, Budapest and a host of other capitals have romantic rivers adding color, life and diversity to their city-scapes, the rivers of Athens – all three of them – have been boxed into concrete channels and buried almost totally out of sight. The Ilissos and Kiphissos suffered this fate in the mid 20th century; the Eridanos, which flowed through the center of Athens, was covered over by the Romans, if not earlier.

And yet it is the Eridanos that makes the Kerameikos more than just an interesting collection of tombs and historic walls. Although it probably was never more than a seasonal torrent, swollen by winter rains and virtually dry in August, its muddy banks were a wonderful source of clay. Which brings us to a chicken-and-egg story: Did the area become the potters' district because this was where the cemetery was located (from the 12th century BC on) or did the cemetery become established there because of the proximity of the potters? Potters were as essential to funerals as morticians are today, since urns were required for grave offerings and as containers for ashes. Unlike the Orthodox Church, the ancients did not consider cremation anathema.

In any case, the district took its name from Keramos, a son of Dionysos and Ariadne and patron of the potters (*kerameis*). Eridanos, on the other hand, was thought to be a minor god, one of the three thousand son-rivers from the union of Oceanos and Tethys, which also resulted in three thousand daughters, the Oceanids. With its source at the foot of Lycabettus, the Eridanos flowed through what is now Syntagma Square; you can see a small section of the petrified bed bristling with shards and behind glass on exhibit in the Metro station. From there its course ran under Philellinon, Othonos and Mitropoleos streets, down Adrianou (where a bit of ancient channel lies exposed) and alongside the tracks at Monastiraki. Then it bends to the northwest and enters the cemetery enclosure, where it surfaces for a few hundred meters before entering another underground channel and eventually joining up

with the cemented bed of the Kiphissos, which parallels Pireos Street.

Granted, this slow-moving trickle is not much to look at. But the fact that it exists at all is remarkable and reflects the symbiosis of archaeology and ecology. Few laws preserve ecosystems that occupy prime real estate in the middle of a burgeoning city, but they do protect ancient monuments and therefore, inadvertently, some vestiges of nature manage to survive in these sites, even when surrounded by heavy traffic and noxious smog.

A booklet prepared by the Ministry of Culture in 2000 catalogues these vestiges, reporting that the Kerameikos is home to fifteen species of birds and animals, one fish – a miniscule creature called the mosquito fish that can cope with the river's shrinking waters – and 188 plant species within its 40,000 square meters. This does not mean that you will see anything more exotic than a tortoise or a caper bush, but I find comfort in the possibility that hedgehogs may be napping in a shady burrow or that the Callas-like trills coming from the branches of a Jerusalem thorn tree are produced by a Sardinian warbler. It is also reassuring that some branch of the government actually cared enough to conduct this census and publish the information in such an attractively produced, impeccably translated edition. What a welcome diversion from the Great Works in Progress that seem to gobble most public resources.

Although the Kerameikos is a park nowadays, in ancient times it was right in the thick of the city. It formed a continuation of the Agora, something that is hard for us to envisage with all the commotion in Ermou Street and Monastiraki separating the two sites today. It was also the western gateway to Athens and where the city's two main roads – the Iera Odos (Sacred Way) and Panathenaic Way – met. Between the two gates stood a magnificent building, the Pompeion, from which processions set off for Eleusis and the Panathenaic festival. I suppose it would be disrespectful to compare it to Macy's in New

York (another parade starting point), but not entirely inappropriate. The *Dromos*, or The Street, which is what the Panathenaic Way was called outside the Kerameikos, was in fact Athens' main shopping arcade. The Dromos connected the Agora with the Academy and was lined with tombs and memorials to celebrated Athenians including Pericles and soldiers fallen in battle (with the exception of the heroes of Marathon). In other words, there seems to have been no thought of sequestering the dead, no fear that the sight of graves could put a damper on a shopping spree.

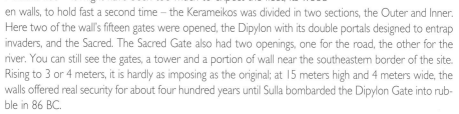

After Themistocles had walls erected around Athens the moment the Persians fled – it might have been too much to expect the fleet, its wooden walls, to hold fast a second time – the Kerameikos was divided in two sections, the Outer and Inner. Here two of the wall's fifteen gates were opened, the Dipylon with its double portals designed to entrap invaders, and the Sacred. The Sacred Gate also had two openings, one for the road, the other for the river. You can still see the gates, a tower and a portion of wall near the southeastern border of the site. Rising to 3 or 4 meters, it is hardly as imposing as the original; at 15 meters high and 4 meters wide, the walls offered real security for about four hundred years until Sulla bombarded the Dipylon Gate into rubble in 86 BC.

For a view of the Kerameikos as a whole, go to the hill, an ancient grave tumulus, opposite the entrance, where there is a map highlighting the various landmarks and monuments. The gates, the Pompeion and the Eridanos are to the right, whereas most of the tombs are to the left. They are far less lavish and flamboyant than the 19th century mausoleums in Athens' First Cemetery, and far less crowded. They come in several styles: *steles* of various degrees of plainness, some with relief portrayals of the deceased; *naiskoi*, where the doleful moment is set in a miniature temple; *aediculae*, where the *naiskos* is but a frame for a relief or a full sculpture; marble urns; and, most common, the *kioniskos*, a slender, undecorated column. There is a whole forest of the latter under the pine trees next to the museum.

In the cemetery's first four centuries the ashes of the dead were placed in urns and then buried, but by the late 8th century BC cremation occurred in the grave itself and urns containing offerings were laid alongside in separate, shallow pits. Gradually markers began to appear, simply inscribed initially, then sur-

Athens' ancient graveyard

mounted with large clay vessels: drinking cups in the case of men (how typically!), two-handled pitchers for married women and single-handled pitchers for virgins. Solon's strict rules restrained the decoration of funerary monuments in the 6th century BC, but it seems that the notion of a tombstone as a measure of social prestige as well as sorrow lies deep within us. By the next century prosperous mourners were commissioning the best sculptors to design ever more ostentatious tombs. We are in awe of steles like the woman with her jewelry box, the Dexileos memorial of a mounted warrior spearing a supine foe, and the sublime statue of a bull that commemorates Dionysos of Kollytos, which are some of the cemetery's most celebrated masterpieces. None postdate the late 4th century BC. That was when the current ruler of Athens, Dimitrios of Phaleron, decided the competition was getting out of control, consuming scandalous amounts of money, and put a stop to it. He decreed that "no tomb shall be built with more elaboration than can be effected by three men in ten days" and that steles should be unadorned and no more than five feet tall. The grave as an art form went out of fashion. Even the potters were reduced to making household goods, since funerary urns were no longer permitted.

Kerameikos is home to fifteen species of birds and animals, and one fish.

Luckily a lot has survived from the pre-puritan period and you can spend hours wandering among the tombs, pondering art and death, or simply enjoying the shade, spring smells and birdsong in this tranquil park. The Oberlander Museum near the entrance, named after its German-American benefactor, contains the originals of some of the most valuable tombstones, dozens of exquisite funerary urns and vases and, most poignantly, many toys that were buried with children: a clay horse on wheels, loaded with four amphorae; birds with elephant feet; a young girl's bracelet and earrings; even a set of knucklebones for playing jacks. The museum needs a facelift, but the exhibits rise above their surroundings.

After I pored over them, I went back to the Eridanos. Its greeny waters were speckled with black tadpoles. Soon they'll be hopping about the banks. But I have since learned, thanks to the Ministry of Culture's wonderful little book, that they are not frogs, but green toads, *Bufo viridis*. ⚪

Practically adjoining the cemetery is a new addition to Athens' long list of excellent museums, the **Museum of Traditional Pottery**. Housed in a beautifully restored 19th century mansion with sumptuously painted ceilings, carved wooden icicles hanging from the roof, and a cobbled courtyard, it would be worth seeing without its exhibits. But these are presented in a lively, informative fashion that cannot fail to please. Using the latest methods including videos, replicas of workshops (with and without the potter's wheel), maps and even microscopes, the museum traces the production process from preparing the clay to firing the glaze. Dozens of examples of household vessels from all over Greece illustrate the period from the early 19th century to the age of plastic. With a café, shop, library and educational facilities that are in constant demand, the museum is the result of decades of collecting by Betty Psaropoulou and the George Psaropoulos Family Foundation. How very fitting that its new home should be in the heart of the ancient potters' district.

The museum, 4-6 Melidoni Street, is open Monday, Tuesday, Thursday and Friday from 9 am to 3 pm, Wednesday from noon to 8 pm, and Sunday from 10 am to 2 pm, admission E2.90, tel. 210 3318491-6.

The Kerameikos,
148 Ermou Street, is open Tuesday through Sunday from 8:30 am to 3 pm, admission €1.50.
Thission is the closest metro station.

1-5 *Grave monuments and ruins in Kerameikos*

Clandestine Byzantine Athens

The Blue Guide gives it only one line: "[Athens] was of little importance in the Byzantine period." A lecturer at the Panorama cultural society confesses, "It's an enigma, a big blank exists between the 3rd and the 15th century." Historians grab at passing mentions in a very few sources, excavations produce more questions than answers. And yet we have the churches. More than a dozen Byzantine churches are scattered around the oldest parts of Athens. They couldn't have just sprung up like anemones with the winter rain. In fact, there used to be many more like them. Seventy-two churches were flattened in the 19th century in the rush to make room for the new capital and 'clean up' the ancient sites. In love with the glory of the Golden Age, no planner, king or archaeologist had a shred of interest in the more recent past.

M ost of the churches still standing date from the 11th and 12th century, and many of them rest on much earlier foundations. As might be expected, Christianity had been slow to find converts in this bastion of Classical thought and knowledge. The early emperors tried to eradicate the pagan religions and the schools of philosophy, but even though the center of the world had shifted to Rome and then to Constantinople, Athens remained an important university town revolving around Plato's old Academy. The first serious threat came in 435 when Theodosius II issued the order to close all the ancient shrines. The Parthenon, with the statue of Athena still in place, was eventually rededicated to the Virgin

and the Hephaisteion to St. George. The Christians also started erecting new buildings, outside the city walls. Evdokia, the emperor's Athenian wife, saw to it that an enormous basilica was constructed near the temple of Olympian Zeus. It was called St. Leonides after an early bishop of Athens but it also commemorated her father Leontius, a sophist philosopher. The lady was obviously torn; though she was a Christian, she respected the old learning. The faculty she later endowed in Constantinople emphasizing Greek rather than Latin scholarship kept the classics alive until the Renaissance.

It was Justinian who delivered the *coup de grace*. He closed the Academy and the other schools in the early 6th century, not with proclamations and barred entrances but simply by stopping their grants. Without money they could not continue and the professors all drifted off to Constantinople. The campaign to discredit the ancient civilization coincided with a series of invasions by Slavic tribes, and Athens must have been a rather sad and surrealistic place. Many of the grand buildings restored by the Romans after the first barbarian attack by the Herulians in the 2nd century AD, almost four centuries earlier, were devastated, along with the humbler residences of the ordinary citizens. And yet during the 8th century, supposedly a bleak period, Athens seems to have recovered somewhat. Two emperors, who never would have picked a gauche provincial, chose Athenian women to be their wives, and a magnificent basilica replaced an earlier church in the courtyard of Hadrian's Library. You can still trace its floor plan superimposed on the foundations of the earlier monument.

By the 10th century, Athens was heading back to prosperity. It had as many as ten bishops and, in 1054, some 140 churches. In 1018, Basil the Bulgar-Slayer had a Te Deum sung in the church of the Blessed Virgin – the Parthenon – to praise God for the victory that gave him his horrific name. It must be said, however, that he had come to do homage to the defenders of Marathon and Salamis, rather than pay his respects to Pericles and Plato. In any event, Athens appears to have been thriving on profits from Hymettus honey, soap, dyes for Theban silks and sculpture, while pilgrims came from all over Europe and the Holy Land to visit the Acropolis and buy relics and souvenirs.

Meanwhile the center of Athens continued to be the agora. The market district functioned in more or less the same way from antiquity until the late 19th century. And because we know where various activities were located during the Ottoman period, we can deduce what was going on towards the end of the Byzantine era. The area around Pandrossou and Hadrian's Library was probably the so-called Upper Bazaar, where there may have been storehouses for agricultural prod-

ucts; the steps off Pandrossou and into Monastiraki formed the Lower Bazaar, with the fabric and tanning industries, the ironmongers and coppersmiths – which are echoed in today's shops – and the barbers, cutting hair on the steps. The Roman Agora seems to have been the place where salt, olive oil and wheat were traded, using the original Roman weights until the late 17th century.

Monastiraki itself takes its name from the Pantanassa Monastery which lay outside the Byzantine city walls. A map drawn in 1820 shows it stretching from the start of Athinas Street, up Ermou and Aiolou. It did survive the War of Independence but not the growth of the city. Many monastery buildings fell victim to excavations in 1868 and the new electric train line installed in 1896 all but obliterated it. The small church in Monastiraki Square was built much later and has been completely deformed by 'restorations'. Pantanassa was a subsidiary of Kaisariani and its nuns were dedicated to helping the poor.

The churches

The city's Byzantine churches are concentrated around Plaka with just a few exceptions. Some have been restored to mint condition, others have suffered from insensitive additions and 'improvements', but every one of these 11th and 12th century buildings can tell us a bit about the last phase of Byzantine Athens.

Take the Russian church on Philellinon Street, for example. Once part of a large convent, Agios Nikodimos was built in 1031, on the site of an earlier church which had been constructed over some Roman baths. It contains marble used in the Classical Lyceum along

Clandestine Byzantine Athens

Agios Nikodimos was built a thousand years ago, on the site of an earlier church which had been constructed over some Roman baths.

with a throne from the theater of Dionysos and its terracotta Cufic designs imitating Arabic script were probably the work of Arab craftsmen. But Turkish cannonballs severely damaged the church in 1827 and it was eventually bought by Tsar Nicholas I for the Russian community here. The Greek state sold it on the condition that restoration would follow the original plan, but somehow the architects failed to comply.

Restoration efforts and sheer neglect have taken a much harsher toll on the Sotira tou Kottaki in its charming garden on Kydathinaion Street. A 12th century church on a 6th century foundation, it had fallen into such disrepair that it was used as a urinal in the last century. So the cheap broken glass in the dome and unsightly window bars are in fact a step up. Here you see the characteristic Athenian dome, which is taller than in Byzantine churches elsewhere and has slim pillars framing each of its arches.

In Agia Aikaterini near the Lysikrates monument, only the octagonal dome and the central apse belong to the original 11th century structure, but it has fared better than its neighbor. Set below street level in a garden boasting five royal palms, some olive trees and a Corinthian capital, it contains features borrowed from Islam – plates tucked into the wall – as well as marble window casements that date back to antiquity. It tops the list for Athenian weddings and its choir is one of the city's best.

The next church is Agios Nikolaos Rangavas on Prytaniou Street. The most amusing way to reach it is by walking up Epimenidou, down Thespidos and then left onto Rangava, a mere path just under the Acropolis past a lovely garden. This church is by far the largest of the city's Byzantine jewels and dates

from the same era as the monastery at Daphni, Kapnikarea and Agia Eleftheria next to the Metropolis, although a good percentage of it consists of later additions. Ancient blocks and columns are clearly visible next to the typically Byzantine brick decoration around the windows. This was the first church in Athens to acquire a belltower after the War of Independence (bells were forbidden in Ottoman territory) and the first to ring freedom in 1944.

Now, if you go down Tripodon to Adrianou, Plaka's main shopping street, peek through the decrepit door at number 96 for a glimpse of the graceful arches fronting the Ottoman era house belonging to the

Clandestine
Byzantine
Athens

29

Benizelos family. Given that St. Philothei was one of its members, you would think the Ministry of Culture would be more interested in restoring this elegant property.

Inside the Agora, Agii Apostoli is the only church that has survived of the nine that once stood here. It was spared the wreckers' ball because of its distance from the heart of the Agora and its exceptional beauty. Outside the dome is supported on a typically Athenian high drum, inside it rests on ancient capitals, as does the altar. The narthex or vestibule contains plans and paintings showing the history of this thousand-year-old church.

Kapnikarea, an island in the middle of Ermou Street, is a familiar landmark. Look closely and you'll see that the original 11th century building dedicated to the Virgin Mother received an addition in the 12th century: the chapel of St. Barbara, which is heavier and less graceful. Five different versions exist to explain the origin/meaning of its name. The word *kapnos* (tobacco or smoke) suggests it may have had something to do with a tobacco officials or an icon that survived fire and smoke. Some scholars think the name derives from *kamouha*, a valuable fabric made in the district, but no one will ever know for sure. Inside, there are frescoes done by Fotis Kontoglou in the 1950s, some beautifully carved modern church furniture, and some 19th century, Western-style paintings. These sentimental, bland works predate a decision taken in the 1930s to have only two-dimensional traditional Byzantine-style icons and frescoes in Greek churches.

After Kapnikarea's synthesis of pointed eaves and rounded arches, the 'Small Metropolis' in the shadow of the Cathedral seems plain, but only from a distance. Instead of the traditional Byzantine brickwork, its walls are marble, decorated with a stunning collection of plaques from earlier buildings. An ancient Greek frieze depicts a calendar of Attic festivals and zodiac signs; below it flat, stylized pairs of birds and winged lions of Eastern origin are placed alongside a medieval cross being saluted by a Classical figure.

Whoever assembled this amalgam of past art must have had great respect for its creators. The church was initially dedicated to the Virgin Gorgoepikoos -- she who grants requests quickly -- but after Independence it was renamed Agia Eleftheria, which literally means St. Freedom.

Who said there was a dearth of information? I've barely skimmed the surface and haven't even mentioned Agii Asomati at the bottom of Ermou or Agii Theodori near Klathmonos Square. But Agios Ioannis on the corner of Evripidou and Koumoundourou streets, beyond the Central Market, deserves at least a line. This was a rural chapel and Ai Yannis had inherited the healing powers of Asklepios. Not much is left of the original structure except a Corinthian column rising above its makeshift roof. In the Middle Ages, the sick used to tie ribbons to it, hoping the saint would cure them; apparently, some people still do.

The past, in all its manifestations, is always present in Greece, but the Byzantine era stopped short in Athens in 1205 after Western Catholic Crusaders parcelled out the empire. That year, when the Franks severed Greece from its roots, can be considered the beginning of the real Dark Ages. As a former bishop exiled to Kea wrote, "You cannot look at Athens without tears."

With thanks to Marietta Konstantinou of the Panorama cultural society for her inspiring lecture and tour.

10

1 *Agios Nikolaos Rangavas*
2 *Small Metropolis, detail*
3 *Lysikrates monument*
4 *Small Metropolis*
5 *Small Metropolis, detail*
6 *Kapnikarea*
7-8 *Agii Theodori*
9 *Agios Nikolaos Rangavas*
10 *Agios Ioannis*

Kaisariani:
one of God's secret gardens

In France there is a tradition that the garden belonging to a monastery or church should be God's garden, devoid of artifice and containing only those flowers and trees that grow in the area naturally. Kaisariani, the 11th century monastery on Mt. Hymettus, is such a place, but there God has had immense help from an Athenian organization called *Filodasiki*, the Friends of the Trees Society, founded in 1904.

Once at the monastery, city cares and cacophonies dissipate into the clear air.

W e know from ancient sources and more modern writers that the piney verdure of the monastery site formed, as the early 19th century traveller Edward Dodwell put it, "a striking contrast with the parched and yellow hue of the Athenian plain," and that was before it was filled with grey concrete and brown smog. But after the Second World War Hymettus was bleak indeed. The Nazis executed Greeks not far from the monastery, and the citizens had chopped down nearly all the pines for firewood. In 1945, Katy Argyropoulou and Vassilis Melas, heads of the Filodasiki, threw all their energies into reforesting a thousand-acre area on the mountain side, leased to the society by the Ministry of Agriculture. In 1952 they began restoration of the long-deserted monastery itself, employing prominent Byzantinologists in a project which lasted ten years.

Three million trees later, the mountainside is glorious, endowing Kaisariani with the shade and serenity of earlier eras, despite persistent attempts by firebugs each summer to reduce it to charcoal. Though the Greek government never supports or even acknowledges the ongoing work of the Friends of the Trees, they routinely dispatch visiting heads of state to admire it, after the obligatory pilgrimages to the Acropolis and Daphne Monastery. Elsewhere, however, recognition has not been lacking. In 1994 the European Union proclaimed the monastery and 6.5-acre garden around it as one of the 58 most important Historic Gardens and Architectural Monuments in Europe, the Society has twice received awards from the Academy of Athens, and in 1997 they won a Henry Ford European Conservation prize.

Once at the monastery, so close to the center of town (maybe a 20 minute drive depending on the

traffic), city cares and cacophonies dissipate into the clear air. Blackbirds hidden in the thick foliage trill unending arias, Judas trees send velvety pink ripples through the dappled shade, flowerbeds sparkle with forget-me-nots bluer than Irish eyes. Unobtrusive landscaping, trashless paths, little log stools to perch on, fountains and, most of all, its variegated greenery, so soothing a respite from the Attic glare, welcome visitors at any time of year.

Athenians have been making pilgrimages up here for centuries. Long before there was a monastery or even a single god, its three springs attracted worshipers. One, the so-called Aghiasmos or Consecrated Water, was the ancient Kallia Fountain, where Ovid placed his tale of the jealous lovers, Cephalus and Procris, in his *Ars Amatoria*, the *Art of Love*. There must have been something more than usually erotic about the spot because a temple of Aphrodite was erected here, and in ancient times women would bathe in the spring, hoping to cure their infertility. When the worship of the Virgin replaced that of Aphrodite, mothers would dip their sick children in its waters instead. John Freely, in his wonderful book, *Strolling Through Athens* (1991), describes a very ancient ritual that occurs every year on the 15th of

Monks no longer mutter their orisons or teach philosophy inside its lovely stone walls – instead, it is drawing new life from its plants.

August, after the mass in celebration of the Assumption of the Virgin: "The clergy lead a procession from the monastery up to the Aghiasmos, where they wait to catch a fleeting glimpse of the dove that descends from heaven and hovers over the spring: this epiphany renews the healing powers of the spring's waters, and all of the faithful thereupon drink from the sacred fountain." Actually, until the construction of the Marathon Dam, much of Athens' drinking water came from this spring, which feeds into the Ilissos River, now a mere trickle buried under asphalt and cement.

The water flows from here down to a fountain carved in the shape of a ram's head near the entrance to the monastery. This curious sculpture, part of a Roman sarcophagus, gave Kaisariani its Turkish name, *Cochbashi*, but no one has been able to pinpoint the origin of the word '*Kaisariani*'. Possible interpretations range from a lady donor named Syriani to an icon hailing from Caesarea in Asia Minor. The monastery itself was founded in the 11th century. (As I write I can still hear the American tourists who asked a friend whether she meant BC or AD!) It was built on the ruins of a 5th century basilica, itself erected atop an ancient secular building. You can see remnants of these and other earlier structures lying in the monastery courtyard or recycled as door lintels or supporting columns.

Snug inside its fortification walls, the monastery consists solely of the church (*katholikon*) dedicated to the Presentation of the Virgin; a bath house; a two-story wing of cells; and the kitchen-refectory, two unadorned, vaulted rooms. A small entrance fee will get you into the church and refectory; the other buildings with their arches, stairways and columned porch are off limits, though you can peer into the bath house, long ago converted into an olive press.

It is worth paying the fee just to feast your eyes on the frescoes inside the church, most of which have been painted against a black background which makes the shades of ocher, brown, robin's egg blue and terra-cotta in the robes, buildings and fanciful landscapes exceptionally vibrant. The paintings are later than the architecture: the oldest in the side chapel dedicated to St. Anthony of Padua, erected under Frankish rule, are from the 14th century, while the others belong to the late 17th-early 18th century and the

Kaisariani:
God's
secret garden

Turkish occupation. The flowing, rounded contours used to depict the various saints and scenes from the life of Christ indicate the frescoes were inspired by Cretan iconography rather than the more stylized, formal Macedonian art typical of Mount Athos.

Though Athens changed hands repeatedly during the life of the monastery, the abbots always managed to secure their independence and, more importantly, freedom from taxation, no matter whether the Franks or Ottomans were in charge. Their privileged status, talent for buying up prime real estate elsewhere in Attica, and skill at raising the bees that had been making Hymettus honey famous since antiquity combined to bring great wealth to the monastery. But the abbots and monks also acquired a reputation as scholars and teachers and Kaisariani became a repository of Greek literature and history for the whole region.

By the end of the 18th century, however, the monastery was moldering, caught in a snare of corruption, loss of privileges and poor administration. In 1824 the city elders wrote that "the convent that could save and enlighten many human souls has now become the abode of animals, oxen, donkeys and horses. The precious parchment manuscripts of the library have been sold to the English and the rest were used by the cooks of the Metropolis." Unfortunately, all of its magnificent library went up in smoke during the siege of Athens when the Turks used the paper from its books as wadding in their rifles.

Today, Kaisariani is experiencing a rebirth. True, monks no longer mutter their orisons or teach philosophy inside its lovely stone walls; instead, it is drawing new life from its plants. Since the end of the war the Friends of the Trees has operated a nursery to back up their reforestation projects and sold surplus shrubs and seedlings to discerning gardeners. Not only has the nursery grown and improved over the years, it is among the few places in the Athens area that specializes in providing wild plants indigenous to Greece, those that are rarely found in commercial garden shops. The variety is quite staggering and, what is more, they now have a catalogue in Greek and in English of all the plants for sale, the conditions they require (sun, shade, dry, moist, etc), and other pertinent information. If you're bored with

African violets and geraniums, come here for hardy rock roses (*cistus*), Cretan irises, and a whole gamut of salvias and herbs. All the plants are grown outdoors in a natural environment and propagated in earth and compost, without hormones, chemical fertilisers or sprays, so you can be sure they are healthy, strong and ecologically friendly.

While growing plants for sale, the Friends of the Trees nursery staff have also been raising others for use in a new project – a botanical garden on a piece of mountainside above the monastery. Starting with the garden begun in 1964 by Katy Argyropoulou – which was more or less abandoned over the years – they have introduced hundreds of species to the hillside. Most are flora indigenous to southern Greece, since northern plants are more similar to those found in the rest of Europe. A delight in almost any season, with several types of peonies, tulips and orchids as well as more common plants, the garden suffered considerable damage in the snowstorms of January 2002. Replanting and staffing problems mean that the garden is only open for group visits by prior arrangement. The nursery, practically a botanical garden in itself, is open Monday to Friday, from 8 am to 1 pm. At any other time of day, you'll have to content yourself with a walk through the glades and groves around the monastery and the view, which Dodwell described as without equal "in rich magnificence or attractive charms." ○

How to get there

Buses leave from the University on Akadimias Avenue for the Athens suburb of Kaisariani. The monastery is about half an hour's walk from the last stop. The buildings are open from 8:30 am-3 pm, except Mondays. Call 210 7231769 to arrange a group visit to the botanical garden.

Where to eat

Although this is a fine picnic spot, there is a refreshment stand on the premises. In less clement weather, head down the hill to the fish tavernas in Kaisariani Square. *Trata*, reportedly the best of them, is famous for its fish soup, grilled langoustines and extravagant salads.

1-5 *Kaisariani Monastery, details*

Treasure hunting in Attica:

A search for humble churches

They're scattered all over the countryside. Simple, whitewashed buildings with weathered tile roofs, low asymmetrical doors, and slits for windows, they are often hardly distinguishable from a shepherd's hut or farmer's storeroom. They seem to have been erected without rhyme or reason for though some of them cap low hills, others simply squat in a flat, mundane patch of field with no walls or trees to highlight their presence. A few of them are extremely old, occupying foundations laid by pagans or very early Christians, but most of these tiny chapels date from middle of the Ottoman occupation, the 17th or 18th century. Turkish rule may have been financially oppressive but religious persecution was not its aim.

'd been wanting to track down some of these forgotten churches for years, decades in fact, ever since I got hold of a book called *Churches of Attica,* which was a best selling coffee-table edition in the early 1970s. Though printed only in black and white, it catalogues the facades, interiors and floor plans of 42 chapels ranging from Megara to Anavyssos. With its publication, the authors, C. Bouras, A. Kalyeropoulou and R. Andreadi, were hoping to alert the public to the sorry state of some of the churches and save their frescoes before mold and neglect damaged them irreversibly.

With so many drastic changes in the Mesogeia district, following their directions almost thirty years after the book's publication met with more than a few hitches. Two or three churches proved impossible to find even with dogmatic assistance from knowledgeable *horta* pickers. "Turn left at the *gymnasio,* never mind if it's a one-way street," they'd instruct us, or "Just keep going until you get to the asphalt road, which will take you right to the Panayia." Some of those which we did find had been 'improved' by the addition of unsightly concrete sheds, some were locked, while others had been lovingly tended and restored. But all of them had an endearing quality: a charming architectural feature, unexpectedly fine wall paintings, an unusual setting. In fact, the mere existence of these churches is something of a miracle and sets you thinking about what Attica must have been like some three or four hundred years ago, when Athens itself was just a village, the Orthodox religion was recovering from Frankish Catholic overlordship, and the Mesogeia's vineyards and olive groves were interrupted only by tiny hamlets.

Because the largest cluster of churches is around Koropi and Markopoulo, we decided to confine our first explorations to this area. The map in the book showed three of them in a line west of Koropi, and though we overshot the "small square with the statue of King Constantine I," where we were meant to turn right, we found the church of Agii Asomati (the Holy Angels) without much difficulty about a kilometer outside town. Its original 17th century cross-in-square configuration, tucked under a tiny dome, has been elongated by a 20th century shed, but the addition has a pleasant lopsided air about it and does not offend. The interior is a commotion of frescoes of red-winged and red-legged angels, faded holy fathers and a Virgin Platytera, arms outstretched to embrace the world.

Next on the list was Agios Athanasios. But where was it? The book's directions were not much help: "The horizon is open, for the country around is uninhabited, and the visitor sees only considerable traces of walls of houses and other piles of stone." Thirty years ago the church might have been obvious amidst the rubble of the medieval village of Filiati, which in turn "was built on the ruins of the deme of Sphettos, one of the earliest and largest in Attica in antiquity." But now abandoned poultry hatcheries, small factories of an unspecified nature, farm houses and even a *villitsa* or two fill the gaps between vineyards and olive trees. A farmer came to our rescue and pointed us down a dirt road to the left of Agii Asomati and there it was – a long shoebox of a church with a small apse at the end, lichen-encrusted tiles, early Christian inscriptions set into the front wall, and a ghastly flat concrete appendage sheltering the entrance. Inside were a score of frescoes with blackened faces, pale but energetic horses, and a scene showing Abraham entertaining the angels with some hounds gamboling beneath the haloed guests.

Our search in this direction had led us to the end of the road where we caught sight of a beautiful unnamed domed chapel tantalizingly out of reach – for this expedition, at least – on the crest of a precipitous hillside. And on heading back into Koropi we passed Agios Petros, doubly padlocked and also 'embellished' by the faithful with a nasty concrete shed. This illustrates a central problem: The State/Ministry/Archaeological officialdom cannot cope with all the treasures littering the Greek countryside, but if their care is entrusted to the community, the locals' idea of what constitutes looking after a historic monument will rarely be appropriate. Alas, the Church itself is no better guardian, as a glance at most modern churches will confirm. Faith and sensitivity to the past seem to be worlds apart.

Driving down Koropi's main street once more, I had the sinking feeling that the landmarks guiding us to the churches on the east side of town would not be easy to locate. "On the left... after the main square, is an old well whose rim bears the marks of centuries of use. From this point exactly, an asphalt road runs east, which is in fact the ancient road to Brauron. After about three quarters of an hour's walk out of the village, at the place called Skouperi, the traveller finds by the roadside, on the left, the unusual church of Sts. Cosmas and Damian." Sadly, no well was to be spied amid the hectic Saturday morning

traffic and crisscrossing the back streets turned up no ancient roads nor churches with 12th century frescoes. Instead, a ghetto of blue and yellow plywood gypsy shanties tacked onto the edge of Koropi left us appalled and sad.

We were on our way to Keratea when I noticed a sign to Kouvara off to the left of the Lavrio-Markopoulo road. This collection of concrete structures masking an old hamlet contains two captivating churches, Agios Georgios and another Agios Athanasios. The latter is even signposted and lies about 3 km outside the village on a back road to Avlaki and Porto Rafti, which starts at the square with the modern church of Agios Demetrios. Agios Athanasios is a little gem that has been cleaned up since 1970, but at the price of sharing its courtyard with a small monastic residence of sorts, garnished with lurid green and yellow window panes. Nevertheless, the church is a marvel of the Turkish period. Its facade is embedded with early Christian reliefs, pocked with the hollows left by a series of purloined Rhodian plates (only one remains *in situ*), and shorn up by old but-

A search for humble churches

tresses as well as iron scaffolding. Inside, a timber ceiling divided by three slender arches adds a log cabin feeling, while the frescoes covering almost all the surfaces, including the arches, give off a reddish-ocher glow. Most of them were painted by an 18th century artist named G. Markos, about

The interior was a commotion of frescoes: red-winged and red-legged angels, faded holy fathers and a Virgin Platytera, arms outstretched to embrace the world.

whom my book is regrettably uninformative but who was responsible for many church interiors in the Markopoulo area. He has a lively style, not as mannered or formal as some more tutored hagiographers, and his narrative scenes pulsate with movement and expression.

These are especially evident in Kouvara's other church, dedicated to St. George, where one whole wall depicts a memorable Last Judgment with hapless sinners and triumphant saints. (To see these frescoes you must get the key from the priest of Agios Demetrios.) This church (head west on Ag. Georgiou road before the entrance to Kouvara as if you were returning to Markopoulo) is longish with a strange buttress at the front and a timber ceiling. Though it looks uniform, it was erected in three stages – during the Early Christian era, around 1000, and in the Turkish period. Early Christian capitals and columns support the later arches.

The last church we found is also easy to spot from the Lavrio-Markopoulo road because it shares a hillside on the outskirts of Markopoulo with a Frankish watchtower. Here the frescoes are much damaged or obliterated by whitewash, but the architecture of the Taxiarchis is a delightful combination of apses, a dome, and angled roofs of different shapes and sizes. Just opposite it, next to the village football field, stands Agios Demetrios, also with a timber roof and Early Christian elements.

In any case, there are more than enough churches for another day's treasure hunt. The twin ocher chapels of Agia Paraskevi and Agia Thekla right in Markopoulo are covered with Markos's frescoes and are open between 10 and 12 and after 5 pm. And we still have to discover the Panayia Varava which has a column drum peering out from one wall like a big blind eye; Agia Triada, a double church with barrel vaulting; and at least eighteen others between Kantza and Kalyvia. Tracking them down will put us in touch with a generation of Attica residents who've been barely noticed between their illustrious Classical ancestors and their TV-watching, pickup-driving descendants. ○

Note
This article was written before the completion of the *Attiki Odos* (Attica Highway), but if you keep to the old roads in the Koropi-Markopoulo area, you should be able to locate most of these churches. The yellow and brown signposts erected by the Archaeological Service are a great help.

Where to eat
The old road between Paiania and Koropi is lined with tavernas specializing in spitted and grilled meats, while there are a couple of decent, old-fashioned tavernas in Markopoulo which serve ready-cooked food.

1-2 *Agios Taxiarchis, Markopoulo*

3,8 *Agios Athanasios, Kouvara*

4 *Agios Georgios, Kouvara*

5 *Agios Athanasios, Koropi*

6 *Agia Paraskevi and Agia Thekla, Markopoulo*

7 *Profitis Ilias*

Piraeus:
more than just a hectic port

He stands alone in the room, his right foot slightly in front of his left, his hands outstretched, his gaze fixed on something within. Though his skin and hair – a few curls plastered to his forehead, long locks tucked behind his ears – are mottled green with age, his body is that of a young athlete with strong thighs and broad shoulders. They say he was a god, Apollo, yet he looks too guileless and innocent for a Greek divinity. I can't take my eyes off him. Yes, he's beautiful, but he's also a technological marvel: the oldest known hollow-cast bronze statue of larger than life size. Sculpted in the last quarter of the 6th century BC, he predates the Charioteer by about 50 years, Poseidon by about 75.

If you keep your eyes open, you'll see beautifully hewn
ancient stones jutting out of modern walls.

In the adjoining room stand other magnificent tall bronzes: a fearsome Athena wearing her owl-tipped helmet, a grimacing Medusa emblazoned on her breast; a robust, serene Artemis no match for any man; a second Artemis looking too feminine and gentle for the role; and a tragic mask, its wild eyes and gaping mouth almost covered by a fleecy mane.

These masterpieces turned up in 1959 when the Piraeus drainage network was being expanded. Archaeologists believe that they had been rounded up by Sulla in 86 BC for export to Rome, but were somehow forgotten – there being so much other booty – and left to molder in a warehouse, which miraculously sank into oblivion instead of being ransacked by future Romans, Goths, Byzantines, Vikings, Venetians or Turks. Now they occupy two rooms in the newly refurbished Piraeus Archaeological Museum, which would be worth a visit even without them.

Not only is the museum beautifully lit, freshly painted and spotlessly clean, its smaller exhibits include things that put a different face on antiquity: a rhyton shaped like a pig's head, vestiges of musical instru-

ments, a 'book' of wax tablets once owned by a poet, children's toys, the wooden (!) lining from a coffin and a terra-cotta figure of a woman contorted in childbirth, breast flapping against her knee. On a larger scale are numerous grave steles, a series of marble reliefs 'mass produced' for a customer in Rome, and an ornate mausoleum from Kallithea in the form of a mini-temple that shelters the portrait statues of a father, son and servant. This was only one of the many monuments that stood before the Long Walls, which stretched from the port to Athens; it represents the apex of funerary sculpture – the Albert Memorial – of the 4th century BC.

I am ashamed to say that over the past two decades or so Piraeus for me has been either a place of transit or the setting for an occasional taverna lunch. Bent double with rucksack, like everyone else I've stumbled out of the old train station (now spruced up for the millennium) and ricocheted through the crowds in what I prayed was the direction of the ferry. Other times, in a car, I've glued my nose to the window and ogled the liners moored under the glass-fronted shipping offices, glanced at the neoclassical Municipal

Theater, and admired a graceful tile-roofed house or two dwarfed by aluminum-balconied *polykats*. If I ever have a moment to spare after the frantic search for a legal parking place within walking distance of the Flying Dolphins, I always spend it inspecting the millionaires' yachts. But this last visit has me thinking I'll become a Piraeus museum junkie.

We happened to be walking from the Archaeological Museum to Zea, in search of ancient walls and docks, when one of our small band of explorers insisted on veering off to the Naval Museum. A low, battleship-grey building at the rear of a scrabbly lawn decorated with anti-aircraft guns and the turret of the Papanikolis submarine, it did not look very inviting. But a glimpse of Themistoclean wall through the window and the adamant refusal of an employee to let us enter within fifteen minutes of closing time whetted our enthusiasm. We made our way to the other end, nudged a second door, and slid into a dark room filled with the shadowy outlines of battleships and liners. Presently the director himself appeared and instead of ordering us out, he switched on all the lights and showed us his treasures.

With the aid of meticulous, beautifully made models – beginning with a primitive raft made of bundled reeds and ending with a supertanker – the museum represents an encapsulated history of boat building in Greece. It's fascinating to see that the Athenian trireme of the 5th century BC so closely resembles the Byzantine dromon of a thousand years later; that a cargo vessel which could have shipped supplies to Alexander's men has the same hull as a 19th century Cycladic *perama*. Replicas of famous ships are here too: the battleships 'Elli' and 'Averoff', and even Nelson's 'Victory', carved out of bone, which once belonged to Aristotle Onassis. Among the artifacts you'll find the architect's specifications for

the Naval Arsenal of Philo (which once stood nearby); it is the earliest known document of its kind.

The museum director made a point of showing us a model of some of the wooden shipsheds that sheltered the Athenian fleet. Constructed in Pericles' time, these lined the shores of all three of the ports of Piraeus. By the mid 4th century BC there were as many as 372 sheds, 196 in Zea, 82 in Munychia (Tourko/Mikrolimano) and 94 in Kantharos, the main harbor, whose name means 'goblet'. Demosthenes praised them in the same breath as the Parthenon and the Propylaea, and they were indeed a measure of the strength of the Athenian navy, which numbered about 400 ships in his day.

Before Themistocles' term as governor, the Athenians used to beach their boats at Faliron, where they could be watched over from the Acropolis. But on the eve of the Persian invasion, Themistocles – heeding the Delphic Oracle – was convinced of the need for 'wooden walls' in the form of a strong navy. He also saw the potential of the coves

Piraeus:
more than
a hectic port

indenting the Akti or Piraeus peninsula, originally an island, for sheltering them. In 493 BC he ordered the building of both ships and defense walls: two sets of Long Walls that ran from the coast to the Pnyx and the City Wall that protected the three harbors and sliced through the peninsula. Even though all three fortification systems were destroyed at the end of the Peloponnesian War, the Long Walls were rebuilt and their outline can still be traced in the electric railway tracks and Pireos Street. (The City Walls, on the other hand, have been all but obliterated by dense development.) In any case, when Piraeus was refortified in the 4th century BC, Konon extended the walls around the whole of Akti, and great stretches of these can still be seen along the rocky coast.

We set out from the Naval Academy at the northwest point to walk them. A section of wall, along with what may be the base of Themistocles' tomb, is within the campus and off limits, but there are enough old stones visible to make anyone happy. Leaping from rock to rock, we reverted to childhood, stopping to take a photo or compare the perfect masonry of the past with the lamentable mediocrity of the contemporary apartment blocks. Eventually we came to Aphrodite's cove where dinghies were pulled up on shore under a chapel dedicated to St. Nicholas, an example of the congruity of pagan worship and Christianity found so often in Greece.

There are other bits and pieces of antiquity scattered about Piraeus, such as the foundations of one of the ancient gates at Plateia Hippodamou, which is considered the 'Monastiraki' of the area and is the scene of a big flea market on Sunday. Twenty years ago 'real finds' were said to turn up here; it's doubtful whether such things exist anymore. The Yacht Club at Tourkolimano occupies the site of a temple of Artemis; Kastella hill once held the acropolis of Piraeus; and 165 steps near the church of Profitis Ilias lead to the Cavern of Arethusa which held the ancient city's water supply. If you keep your eyes open, you'll see more and more beautifully hewn stones jutting out of modern walls or hidden behind basement windows.

But we decided to enjoy the present and spend the rest of the glorious springlike day ingesting seafood and 'grape juice'. Smells of frying fish and grilling octopus soon lured us up from Konon's walls onto the corniche, where every taverna offered possibilities. On terra incognita, we chose the most crowded, squeezed around a table and were soon tucking into mountains of crisp *barbounia* (red mullet) and shrimps, emptying carafes of pale ambrosial retsina and mopping up olive oil and feta crumbs with thick slices of sesame-crusted peasant bread. *La vita è bella.* Especially on a sunny Saturday in Piraeus. ◯

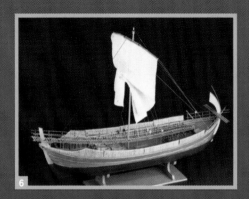

Note
The Piraeus Archaeological Museum, Harilaou Trikoupi 31, is open Tuesday-Sunday from 8:30 am to 3 pm, while the Naval Museum at Zea is open from 9 am to 2 pm, Tuesday-Saturday.

Where to eat

There is no dearth of wonderful restaurants and tavernas in Piraeus. *Dourambey's* near the canal opposite Peace and Friendship Stadium is famous for its fried *karavida* (scampi) tails, impeccably fresh clams and oysters and marvelous salads, but it's quite pricey. *Mandraki*, close to the entrance to Zea, is an old favorite with excellent fish and wine. One of the simplest and most agreeable tavernas is just outside the gates of the Naval Academy. The fare is limited. Fried shrimps and red mullet, salad, feta and wine are all that's on offer, but the quality is superb. Go early to get a table; this is a very popular place.

1-5 *Bits of old wall are easy to spot in Piraeus.*
  6 *Ship model*
  7 *Tragic mask*

Marathon's hidden monuments

Almost seven hundred years after the battle of Marathon, in the 2nd century AD, Pausanias wrote that "every night you can hear the noise of whinnying horses and of men fighting" on the plain. He also cautioned his guide book readers that "it has never done any man good to wait there and observe this closely, but if it happens against a man's will the anger of the daemonic spirits will not follow him."

The plain where the historic battle was fought breeds cabbages, leeks and summer bungalows.

Today the strip of land between the sea and the low bare mountains where the historic battle was fought breeds cabbages, leeks and summer bungalows. Daemonic spirits seem long vanished and even the material reminders of antiquity are all but engulfed by the construction that has overtaken the district in the past three decades. Some of its ancient sites are impossible to find, others are concealed in locked

sheds or disfigured by rubbish. Nevertheless, tracking them down is like going on a treasure hunt even if the treasure may prove somewhat elusive.

Most of us remember Marathon because it inspired a lot of running. When the Persian fleet was spotted sailing up the coast from Karystos, the Athenians dispatched Pheidippides to rally the Spartans. After the battle another young man ran the 24 miles back to the city to announce the Greek victory. Although his exertions killed him, rather than acting as a deterrent, they have inspired countless professionals and Sunday joggers to repeat his act in various unlikely places from Boston to South Africa, several times a year. But I think the less well known soldiers' walk is even more inspiring.

Picture this the next time you drive over poor charred Penteli to unleash the dog or take a wintry dip at the sickle-shaped beach at Schinias: Bobbing in the bay, dragged up on the sand, are dozens of Persian galleys. Under the pines, 24,000 troops are bivouacked. It's September, and their cotton uniforms and wicker shields are piled against the trees. Ethiopian archers are flexing their bows and the cavalry are watering their horses at the brackish lake near the far end.

Meanwhile, some 9,000 Athenian soldiers with bronze breast plates are honing their spears and swords for the umpteenth time at the foot of Mt. Agrieliki around a shrine dedicated to Hercules, which

51

controled the only road. For four days their ten generals have been debating whether to wait for the Spartans or strike without them. Finally a civilian is called in to break the stalemate. Kallimachos listens hardest to Miltiades, who's fought Persians before, and gives him command. As they argue, another thousand men arrive from Plataia, a little city-state not far from Thebes on the other side of Attica. Miltiades gives the order to creep up on the Persian encampment, under cover of trees, so the soldiers lop off branches and, rather like Birnam Wood moving to Dunsinane, lessen the gap between the two armies.

On September 12, 490 BC, Ionian deserters rush to Miltiades with unhoped-for information: the Persian cavalry has disappeared, perhaps bogged down in the marshes behind the beach. No one will ever know what happened to them. The Athenian hoplites charge, surprising the Persians. They slay 6,400 of them in the early morning, their long spears slicing through the flimsy shields and padded cotton. Only 192 Greeks die in the melee. It was said that they had help from both Pan and Theseus. The Persians skedaddle, clamber aboard their ships and sail down the coast towards Sounion. The runner sprints off with his joyful news.

The Athenian troops followed the runner, their armor clanking, and marched past Athens to the port where they met the Persian fleet.

5

But what happens next is even more remarkable. The victorious army does not lie down to rest or prepare a barbecue on the beach to congratulate themselves and thank the gods. Instead they follow the runner up the mountain, their armor and weapons clanking, and march past Athens all the way to the beach-port at Faliron. They arrive just before the Persian fleet, which does not even contemplate landing but turns tail for Asia Minor, prestige heavily tarnished. If we were ever to reenact that battle, how many would volunteer to play the soldiers' role?

The heroes' tombs are all that can be seen of that long day. Ordinarily, Athens buried its warriors in state near what came to be known as Plato's Academy at Kolonos. But in homage to their incredible courage, this time

Marathon's hidden monuments

they voted to cremate the bodies at the battle site. There are two funerary mounds, one for the Athenians, the other for the Plataians. Pausanias could find no grave for the Persians and thought the victors must have "carried them to a pit and thrown them in anyhow." The Athenian tumulus is the larger and used to be inscribed with the names of those interred within. The site, clearly signposted and preceded by a spacious carpark, is peaceful and prettily landscaped with olive, plane and cypress trees. A token fee will gain you access and the right to climb up the 10-meter-high slope to the top, despite a sign to the contrary. The grassy mound has a deep brown crease worn in it from the many feet that have ignored the prohibition to do so at the entrance. From there it is said that one can see the battlefield, but vegetable patches and orange groves made it impossible for me, at least, to envisage any violence at all.

The Plataians' mound lies further north along the road towards Schinia and is also clearly marked. It is part of the Marathon museum enclosure, which can be visited with the same ticket. Here is where the treasure hunt becomes frustrating. In the mid 70s, when I was first exploring the area, the Plataian tomb had just been excavated and the vaulted stone chamber was open to the public. Now the entrance corridor leads only to a padlocked door. Behind the museum is an unsightly shed with an aluminum roof. In those days we used to spend hours poring over the complex of prehistoric grave circles inside it. The skeletons of men, women, children and even a horse lay in their earthen boxes separated from us only by plate glass panels. Now by standing on a pile of stones you can peer through two grimy windows for a glimpse of the immaculately cleaned mounds. And that is all.

The first three rooms of the museum proper contain the finds from all these and later graves: spare Cycladic idols, red and black figure pottery from the 5th century BC and Classical steles but, surprisingly, no armor or weapons. There are chunks of neolithic pottery from Pan's cave at nearby Oinoe and a massive Ionic column capital which was part of a victory trophy set up by the Athenians. The modest museum's last two rooms hold a few mysterious vestiges of Marathon's most famous citizen, Herod Atticus. Among them are three sections of the monumental gateway to his estate, dedicated to eternal harmony, two headless herms that stood on the property, and a couple of oversized Egyptian-looking statues he commissioned for a temple to Isis. At the entrance a map dotted with symbols indicates all the ancient places in Marathon, from prehistoric to Roman and Byzantine.

Following Nikis street, a dirt lane between the main tumulus and Schinia beach, we hoped to find the watchtower with some more of the victory trophy embedded in its walls. There was no sign of it as we meandered along patch after patch of perfect lettuces, bulbous cabbages and ruddy beets. Instead we found turbaned Sikhs weeding them and gentlemen in Nehru tunics peddling on bicycles. South of the museum, the path to the chapel reputed to be the site of Hercules' shrine was littered with broken glass, plastic sheets and construction rubble. We were eventually rewarded with a hillside polka-dotted with yellow and white crocuses plus the occasional pale, premature anemone, but no old stones.

Searching for Herod Atticus was marginally more successful. Born around AD 101, Herod inherited a treasure his father happened to find on the Marathon estate. Some say it was Persian loot, others maintain it was the family fortune his grandfather had hidden out of reach of the Roman emperor Domitian. In any

Marathon's
hidden
monuments

case, Herod liked spending it and no doubt we would have called him vulgar and nouveau riche for being so ostentatious. In addition to the Marathon estate, he had a villa in Kifissia and another near Tripoli, which is only now under excavation. His public works have survived better; his theater houses the Athens Festival, his stadium – clad with a year's supply of marble from his own quarry in Penteli – hosted the first Olympic Games in 1896 and is still used for ceremonies. But what about his 'Egyptian' temple?

To find it, we turned onto Kefallinias street just south of the Nea Makri military base and drove down to the sea. The coast there has been landscaped and an asphalt path perfect for roller-blading parallels the narrow beach as far as the uninteresting chapel of Agia Kyriaki. Near it, a convenient hole in an otherwise stout Greek fence led through the underbrush to the temple foundations and the basins and brickwork of some contemporary Roman baths. The site is so obscure that I surprised not only a great green lizard but also a woodcock, that shyest of birds. There was no hint of where Herod's Egyptian-esque statues would have stood, but the discovery of ruins in so unlikely a spot pleased me tremendously.

My quest for Herod's estate, however, ended at the barbed boundary of the Naval Helicopter base on the plateau above the plain. All I could tell was that the plutocrat would have had a magnificent view.

I wondered whether he thought much about the Athenians and Plataians who gave their lives to keep Greece from barbarian rule, and changed the course of Western civilization. I wondered whether the Sikhs and Pakistanis running those market gardens had any inkling of how ironic their presence here is: Easterners feeding Athenians from Greece's most famous battlefield. Did I find the treasure? I certainly had fun looking. ⭕

Where to eat

Fish lovers will find beautifully cooked fresh fish and octopus, better-than-average greens and salads and excellent barrel wine at *Glaros*, at the middle of Schinias beach (signposted). It is owned by triplets, which makes identifying your waiter a bit confusing. *Glaros* is open every day from May through October and on sunny winter weekends. As for meat, there are tavernas galore on either side of the main road between Nea Makri and the turn for Schinias and a cluster of them on the road that parallels the beach before the turn for *Glaros*. As we went to press many of these establishments were in danger of being bulldozed in view of the forthcoming Olympics, since they had been erected without building permits.

The Marathon museum is open until 3 pm daily except Monday. If you can get together a group and call 2294 055155 ahead of time, they may be persuaded to unlock the prehistoric tomb shed for you.

1-2 *The Tumulus, Marathon*
3-4 *The Roman baths*
5 *Frankish watchtower*
6 *Chapel near Marathon*
7-8 *The Marathon area is full of anonymous antiquities.*

Amphiaraion:
Attica's ancient healing center

Nestled at the bottom of a gentle ravine surrounded by a pine forest that has somehow survived the annual infernos that sweep the hills above Oropos, the shrine of Amphiaraion features on few tourist itineraries. A small, mostly Hellenistic site to a now forgotten minor god, it was nevertheless chosen with the unerring sense of place so evident in virtually every ancient holy spot in this country.

Though it takes less than 30 minutes to drive there from Kifissia, I hadn't visited Amphiaraion since that sultry June afternoon some twenty years ago when we maneuvered a harpsichord down the stony path to its theater to give an illicit performance of *Dido and Aeneas*. While we were warming up, friends and fans who had caught wind of this crypto Athens Singers concert trickled in, arranging their cushions, picnic baskets and demijohns on the hummocks and clumps of stone where the seats should have been. After all, no audiences had sat there for at least seventeen hundred years. As we joined our voices to the tinkles and thumps of the harpsichord, Purcell's tunes woke up the nightingales, owls and crickets. Their choruses almost drowned us out, and in the end they stole the show. We lingered to listen to them until the midsummer moon rose and the guard had to go home to his wife.

Now a formidable fence encircles the site and the guard is no longer amenable to such infringements, but the shrine has not lost its magic. And the clearing away of some underbrush has made it seem larger, leaving more to explore. It was dedicated to Amphiaraos, a Bronze Age king of Argos whose ability

Amphiaraos led the attack on Thebes after the Oedipus scandal and was famed for his ability to interpret dreams.

to interpret dreams inspired widespread worship by the Classical era. Amphiaraos was one of the seven kings who led the attack on Thebes after the Oedipus scandal. He went most reluctantly since he had foreseen his own death; and die he did, though not on the battlefield. Rather than let him be slain by a Theban warrior, Zeus opened a chasm in the earth which swallowed Amphiaraos, as well as his horses, chariot and charioteer, for good measure. The alleged chasm seems to have been somewhere between Thebes and Oropos.

Hundreds of years later, the Greeks who held great store by oracles erected several shrines to the legendary seer-hero, and by far the most famous was the one near Oropos, from whose spring he was said to have reappeared as a god. Today there are few traces of that very ancient port city at the modern ferry landing of Skala Oropou, but even in Pausanias's time, there was nothing "great to record." Which was probably why the Oropiotes were so proud of their one attraction, the Amphiaraion, a big money maker. Its prestige and profits surely whetted Athenian appetites for acquisition, for both town and sanctuary were coveted by Athens and Boeotia, who struggled over them for generations.

The shrine was founded in the late 5th century BC and already by the 4th century it was a thriving spa/religious center with a temple, a long colonnade, baths, hostels, shops and, of course, the theater. Now as then a stream runs through it, separating the show-case buildings to the left of the entrance from the smaller residental and commercial ones on the right. The jumbled foundations of the latter have only recently been disentangled from the thick woods and underbrush that concealed them in the days when I used to make my pilgrimages. In fact, we had no inkling of their presence then, but loved to scramble up the opposite bank of the stream to admire the state of the art technology of the Hellenistic era – a water clock. It's a little jewel. A rectangular 'box' about 2 meters deep set inside a larger square equipped with a small flight of stairs, it is a perfect example of the stone cutter's art, as well as being a timepiece more reliable than a sundial. Perhaps it was used to schedule cures, sacrifices or events at the games. Time in those days was refreshingly imprecise, with no onus attached to not being 'on time' or 'in' it.

For about six hundred years the sanctuary was a favourite recourse for people seeking a solution to a problem or relief from an illness. The procedure was simple. After paying the entrance fee, the patient

sacrificed a ram on the altar, which Pausanias says was divided up into sections, each sacred to a diverse group of deities, ranging from Jason and Hercules, to Zeus, Apollo, Athena and Aphrodite, plus Pan, the nymphs and two river gods in addition to Amphiaraos. What a luxury to be able to take one's pick. The pilgrim, wrapping himself up in the fleece of the ram, would then go to sleep, hoping for a portentous dream, in the colonnade, which was lined with marble benches. After interpretation of the dream and any further treatment, which usually included baths in the miraculous waters, it was customary to thank the gods by throwing gold and silver coins into the stream. Needless to say, the priests encouraged this practice; they regularly fished them out and melted them into material for *ex votos* which they could sell at a good profit. The altar must have resembled the icon of the Virgin Mary in Tinos, so bedecked was it with symbolic images of children or afflicted body parts – legs, arms, eyes, breasts. Many such offerings have been found, made of both clay and precious metals.

Like many religious centers of the ancient world, the Amphiaraion celebrated festivals in the form of games, the Lesser Games annually and the Greater Games every five years. It is hard to imagine this secluded spot ringing with the cries of athletes, actors, dancers, musicians, poets, spectators and the inevitable hawkers of souvenirs and refreshments. The space between the stream and the stoa, where the spectators sat, barely seems large enough to have served as a stadium, and the

Attica's ancient healing center

61

wrestling, boxing, pentathlon and other competitions would have had to have been squeezed in there too. At least they did not try to hold the chariot races in the sanctuary proper; the hippodrome was located somewhere on the hill above.

After the sports events, the theater would fill up for plays and poetry readings. It must have been bursting to capacity since it only held 300 seats, plus five beautifully carved marble

For about six hundred years the sanctuary was a favorite recourse for people seeking a solution to a problem or relief from an illness.

thrones placed in the orchestra for VIPs or priests. By the 1st century BC these would have been reserved for Roman dignitaries. The Oropiotes did not welcome the new world order, but because etiquette demanded that they erect statues to their new rulers at great expense, they resorted to recycling.

To the left of the entrance to the sanctuary is a row of more than thirty pedestals for statues, on which whole texts have been minutely and, by now, illegibly inscribed. At one time, they bore the images of wealthy citizens, notable priests or happy patients, but some of their names were obliterated to make space for the obligatory Roman officials. Among them are a few of the famous, including Brutus, whose murder of Julius Caesar made him quite the hero in Greece. The telltale date 240 BC is all that indicates his pedestal (and possibly even his statue) once belonged to an earlier local. ○

How to get there

To get to Amphiaraion, take the national road north, turn right at Malakassa for Markopoulo, and right again at the sign for Sanctuary of Amphiaraos (3 km) and Kalamos. The KTEL buses for Markopoulo/Kalamos leave from Mavrommateon Street near the Archaeological Museum in Athens (tel: 210 8213203), but do not pass the site, so be prepared for a 4 km walk along a tree-lined road, parts of which are disagreeably decorated with litter and rubble.

Where to eat

The peaceful, usually empty site is ideal for pic-nicking but if you'd prefer a taverna lunch, back-track to the Markopoulo road and head down to the village. Where the road widens is a cluster of shops, including *D. Tsakona's psistaria,* where lambchops will be grilling on the coals. The food is the classic bare minimum – meat, salad, *horta*, feta, and genuine fried potatoes – but it's well prepared, the wine is good and it's very cheap. There are several fish tavernas at Skala Oropos and Agii Apostoli, but for a less hectic ambience, drive north along the coast to Dilessi. This is by far the most attractive of the seaside summer colonies, with a handful of traditional fish taver-nas and a landscaped, car-free promenade on the water's edge.

Note

Sadly, the fire of 2000 ravaged the trees on the upper hillsides, while the heavy snow of January 2002 caused further damage, uprooting and breaking pines and olives. But apart from losing two large pines, the sanctuary itself remains unscathed.

The Sanctuary is open daily from 8 am to 2:30 pm, except Mondays. There is a fee of €1.50, which is waived on Sundays and holidays.

6

1	Statue pedestals
2	Water clock
3, 6	The stoa
4	View of site
5	The Theater

Paiania:
a cave, a house, a garden

I have fond memories of Paiania. Of picnics with good friends, three-hour lunches in Kanakis taverna, and walks through hillsides dappled pink with anemones in March or pungent with fumes from fermenting grapes in September. Then it was a modest village with farmhouses barely straddling the road to Markopoulo and Lavrion. Twenty years on, villas and apartment blocks dwarf the few remaining low tiled roofs in town. They sprawl up the stark eastern face of Mt Hymettus and speckle the hills looking south over the Mesogeia Plain and the reddish bald patch streaked with airplane runways. Even Kanakis taverna is no more.

The cave was only discovered in 1926, by a shepherd who lost a goat to the mountain. The goat miraculously survived the 35 meter fall from above.

I t was in Paiania, Demosthenes' birthplace, that I first heard about the special Greek use of doubletalk when dealing with real estate. Some friends had just bought a piece of land on the green slope opposite the village. The sale had been conducted in one of the owners' houses – for there were many and negotiations had gone on tortuously for months. Everyone gathered for the official transaction in the *saloni* where papers were produced, recited and duly signed, and the declared purchase price changed hands in the presence of officialdom. That settled, the party adjourned into the kitchen where a second set of envelopes was passed around – the undeclared supplement – while the notary and the lawyers discreetly lingered behind with the antimacassars and the upholstery. Then the retsina started flowing, glasses clinked together in toasts, and one crafty old peasant cackled, "Well, you may have my land, but I haven't sold you the fruit of my olive trees or the right to sit in their shade!"

But most of all, Paiania to me meant Jaqueline Tyrwhitt and Sparoza, her house and garden on Sparrow Hill off the road to Spata. Jacky and I shared an office at the Athens Center of Ekistics, where she edited a scholarly magazine which provided the intellectual foundation for the commercial architecture and planning projects of Doxiadis Associates. Then in her seventies, Jacky had taught at the Association for Planning and Regional Reconstruction in London and had been a professor of city planning and urban design at Harvard for fourteen years, but her first degree was in horticulture. And at Sparoza, on land bought for as little as 9 drachmas a square meter in 1962, she created a marvelous Mediterranean garden. The hillside was rocky. The thin soil cover could support nothing taller than rockroses, thyme and prickly scrub (she would have known the Latin names), but in the first three years she planted 300 trees in holes blown out with dynamite and filled with good earth. By the time I knew it, her garden represented a collection of plants and shrubs from all over Greece, as well as Australia, South Africa and Italy. She would invite us to watch the moon flower unfurl its single bloom of the season and was especially proud of her mandrake, espied upon a trip to Delos and reintroduced into Attica, where it was once a common weed. Whether wild and indigenous or exotic and imported, Jacky looked after her cultivations with equal care, for she envisaged Sparoza as a nature reserve.

Jacky had no children, but there is no question that she had future generations in mind when she planned her garden. Far from reclusive, she delighted in company, whether in the form of ex-students from Belgrade to Tokyo or villagers from around the corner, and her Kathara Deftera parties were a legendary mix of poets, artists, architects, musicians and ordinary folk of all ages. When she died in 1983, she left her property to the Goulandris Museum of Natural History, where she had made the most systematic and thorough study of Greek flora that its founder Niki Goulandris had ever witnessed. Though the museum could not afford to look after it as a true botanical garden, Sparoza has recently acquired a new circle of friends, caretakers and admirers as headquarters of the Mediterranean Garden Society, founded in 1995. Whenever I go there for a plant sale or meeting, I can almost sense Jacky's elfin smile stretching into a delighted grin somewhere behind the dark blue salvia or amongst the rosy pomegranates, tickled pink that her work and joy are still appreciated.

If love of the Greek landscape is the hallmark of Sparoza, love of Greek traditional crafts and creativity has spurred Ion Vorres's two museums-in-one in Paiania proper. Purists might find the mix of ancient objects, terra-cotta roof ornaments, Byzantine church artifacts and modern art too eclectic; aesthetes might fault some of the works on display as being less than brilliant, but no one can deny that the Vorres

A love of Greek
traditional crafts
and creativity
spurred Ion Vorres
to build two
museums-in-one
in downtown
Paiania.

Paiania:
a cave, a house
a garden

museum is a splendid show. You can almost think of it as a Greek theme park – a homage to what Vorres considers the very best of Greek tradition. And it is certainly a relief from the banal, ugly cement-scape that covers too much of Attica.

In the mid 1960s, Vorres, who had inherited a vast estate in Maroussi, started to convert a ruined stable and two early 19th century village houses into a series of courtyards, public and private rooms to hold a remarkable and growing collection of just about everything made in Greece before the 20th century. He salvaged many treasures from abandoned or about-to-be-destroyed churches and olive oil factories, including what must be the largest assemblage of millstones ever accumulated. You see them used as outdoor tables or as relief scultures inserted into walls in threes or singly. Ponderous stone mortars and troughs, squat lidded jars with earlike handles, polished marble wellheads – upended in a flowerbed – plaques with coats of arms, lion-headed waterspouts and ancient bits and pieces are tucked into various spots around the garden in such profusion that you're barely aware of the dense greenery that serves as their backdrop. The guide claims there are 3,500 trees and plants in this garden, but she whisked us around too quickly for us to challenge this astounding figure.

Inside the house are several more millstones and old implements, solid oaken tables and chairs studded with huge nails that once served as mansion or monastery doors, commemorative china plates brought in by seacaptains in the last century, gilded altarpieces, paintings of great moments in Greek history like the opening of the Corinth Canal or the raising of the flag of liberation at Agia Lavra in 1821 and much, much more. What you will not see here is any Louis XV or Chippendale furniture, Aubusson carpets or Sevres porcelain.

For as Ion Vorres told us as our tour of the house ended, "I've even put rag rugs on the floors, because I want to promote Greece in all its aspects. I don't understand this xenomania that seems to have overtaken my countrymen, the need to knock down our heritage and erect anonymous apartment blocks in its place."

Vorres's admiration for the Greek spirit is by no means restricted only to the past, for the second half of his museum – the stunning sculpture courtyard and the modern gallery – is dedicated to postwar art. If you know nothing about contemporary Greek painting, this gallery will give you a crash course. All the leading names are represented here with at least one trademark work, so there's a big Moralis abstract canvas, a Gaitis cloned bourgeois mensch, a Tsarouchis portrait, a Vassiliou landscape of Eretria, a Pavlos paper fantasy, a Ghikas cubist composition, an Opi Zouni op art piece, and dozens more.

More modern sculpture is scattered about Paiania, for as a two-term mayor, Vorres endowed the town with eye-catching works, from a perforated metal globe to a shiny red, restored steamroller. Under his leadership Paiania also received three hundred trees, new schools and a covered gym.

Another Paiania landmark is entirely nature's work. This is the 4,000 sq. m cave near the top of Mt Hymettus and filled with stalactites and stalagmites. The guide is only too eager to point out resemblances to… the Statue of Liberty, the throne of Zeus, a baboon, a church organ, and the inevitable phallus, but the canyons and corridors, vaults, columns and multicolored walls formed at the rate of a centimeter a year are impressive enough without the commentary and the Vivaldi bubbling through the chambers. Unlike many Greek caves, this one was never used by the ancients to worship chthonic deities. It was only discovered in 1926 by a shepherd who lost a goat to the bowels of the mountain. Hearing it bleat from deep underground he enlisted the help of a well expert from Keratea who happened to be in the *kafeneion* when he related his tale. The man lowered himself 35 meters into the cavern and rescued the goat, which miraculously had survived the fall. Eventually the cave was explored, fitted out with a cement path, illuminated and opened to the public. ○

Information

The Vorres museum is open on weekend mornings from 10 am-2 pm, €4.40, children €2.10, tel. 210 6642520. The Hymettus Cave, run by the GNTO is open daily from 9 am-4:30 pm, adults €4.40, children €2.40. To Kellari, also open on weekday evenings, can be reached at 210 6643216. And anyone interested in learning more about the Mediterranean Garden Society or wishing to visit the gardens at Sparoza may call Sally Razelou at 210 6643089.

How to get there

At the Stavros junction with Mesogeion Avenue turn east for Paiania, which is about 10 km down the road. Both the cave and the Vorres Museum are signposted.

Where to eat

Kanakis having closed, a satisfying end to all these stimuli would be lunch at *To Kellari*, a self-proclaimed "*mousiako* (museum) *tavernaki*," where you will eat and drink extremely well by a roaring fire surrounded by rustic memorabilia and folk art from the recent past. Signs to the taverna begin at the Paiania cemetery, which you will see as you descend from the cave. They lead you through an exceedingly dismal stretch of litter and mess, but your meal will more than restore your good spirits. Otherwise, the main road between Paiania and Koropi has no dearth of acceptable roast lamb joints on Saturdays and Sundays.

1 *The cave*
2 *Vorres Museum*
3-4 *The Sparoza garden*
5 *Vorres Museum, millstones*

Brauron:
Artemis's shrine in the Airport's shadow

Artemis would be pleased. The chaste goddess who was nature's protectress would find the area around her ancient shrine at Brauron or Vravrona, untouched by the plot to convert eastern Attica into a world-class transportation hub. Although it is surrounded by unprecedented development – the raw plain bulldozed for the Spata airport, cement monoliths outside Markopoulo about to support cloverleaf overpasses, and the insistent creep of Porto Rafti's holiday fringe inland – Vravrona still looks the way the rest of the Mesogeia once did.

Vravrona still looks the way the rest of the Mesogeia once did.

Vineyards and orchards cover the fertile flat-lands, olives and pines muffle the contours of the rolling hills. Barely legible placards, flapping from flimsy stands, hint at bargain prices for last year's figs, apricots and peaches. On this March day the bare grey branches have only just acquired green tips and rosy buds, but canary yellow mustard and blindingly white daisies liven up the roadsides despite the lack of rain this spring. This corner is so bucolic, it's hard to imagine it being terribly different in Classical times.

Brauron, to use its original name, is however much older than that. It was one of the twelve communities in Attica that Theseus incorporated into the State of Athens. The tyrant Peisistratos had property here. And there was a neolithic settlement on the hill above the shrine, which is said to have been founded by Iphigeneia, the daughter of Clytemnestra and Agamemnon.

You remember the story. Agamemnon had been showing off as usual. To impress the armies gathered from all over Greece on the pretext of rescuing his brother's wife from Troy, he boasted that he was as great a hunter as Artemis. In those days disparaging a goddess was no laughing matter and she punished him where it hurt most, by becalming the Greek ships on the eve of their departure from Aulis, in northeast Attica. Finally, after months of praying and no doubt much grousing, the Mycenaean king decided to sacrifice his daughter, Iphigeneia, on the advice of a seer who told him nothing else would mollify Artemis. Hearing the startling news that Achilles had chosen her for his bride, the poor girl rushed north from the Peloponnese only to find herself at the center of quite another sort of ceremony. At the last minute, as the knife was being sharpened, Artemis swooped in to the rescue – a *déesse ex machina*? – substituted a stag for the girl and spirited her off to Tauris. Iphigeneia ruled as her chief priestess in that barbarous land where all strangers ended up as sacrifices on the altar of Artemis, until by happy coincidence her brother Orestes appeared. They recognized each other in time to avert another disagreeable execution and escaped from Tauris, taking with them the wooden statue of the goddess, which they installed either at Brauron or nearby Loutsa (where there was also a sanctuary of Artemis). (Of course, the Spartans maintained that Orestes founded the shrine of Artemis Orthia down there, but that is another story.)

As the centuries passed, the character ascribed to the goddess changed and the Artemis worshipped at Brauron was the protectress of agriculture as well as untamed nature, athletics as well as archery, feminine handicrafts like weaving and, most importantly, childbirth. After all, Artemis had helped her mother Leto deliver her twin brother, Apollo. Iphigeneia, also a virgin (and no wonder, after the way her father treated her), became associated with difficult child-bearing and therefore the protectress of children whose mothers had died. Brauron became an orphanage.

Whatever the mythology, the sanctuary at Vravrona postdates the Mycenaean civilization even though a cave there was revered as Iphigeneia's tomb. It seems to have become popular around the 6th century BC, probably the result of efforts by Peisistratos to increase the value of his own real estate in the vicinity, and flourished into the Hellenistic period. By the early 20th century the columns had toppled and most of the sanctuary was covered by a swamp; only the name survived, giving archaeologists a clue to its past.

The most prominent building rescued from the sludge was a large colonnade or stoa, which has been partially restored. This was divided into rooms, each of which held built-in tables and eleven beds lined up along the walls, where the children slept. Of the Doric temple, which stood on a rock 'platform' to the right of the entrance, only a few cours-

What makes it so special are its exhibits, which have to do with women and children rather than kings, warriors and palatial life.

es of the foundations remain. Behind it is the incongruous but picturesque sight of a small domed church, a relic from the 16th century. To the left a rare specimen of a 5th century BC bridge looks like a checkerboard, utterly flat. Though the sanctuary included several other buildings, they have yet to be discovered.

While the shrine is peaceful and charming, a delightful retreat, the Vravrona museum is an overlooked treasure trove. Confusingly, it lies around the next bend in the road and if you don't know it's there you might drive on by. It was designed to be unobtrusive and age has camouflaged it further. What makes it so special are its exhibits, which have to do with women and children rather than kings, warriors and palatial life. There are statues, many of Artemis, naturally, but even more of boys and girls, some holding pets, a rabbit or a bird, for example. Votive offerings – of lamps, vases, bowls – are often doll-house size, while miniature vases and funerary oil flasks are often painted with scenes of girls dancing – as they did at the festivals in honor of the goddess. There are mirrors, beads and loom weights in unusual shapes, all very feminine. Display cases filled with painted shards leave one mesmerized by the modernity and talent of their artists; heads and horses, torsos and profiles that could have been sketched by Tsarouchis, Fassianos or Picasso.

What we don't see are the clothes that were dedicated to Artemis. Women who had had an easy birth gave her lovely garments which were kept in a special wardrobe and perhaps worn during rituals like the "sacred hunt" or the annual festival in which her orphans and other young women performed a dancing bear act. This curious custom derived from one of those provocatively obscure oracles. It seems that to escape an epidemic, Athenians "should not allow a virgin to live in the same house as a man before she had acted like a bear in honor of the goddess." Eventually Artemis's girls were referred to as "bears" (*arktoi*).

Besides finds from Brauron, the museum also contains wonderful pottery with meanders, swastikas and many unfamiliar motifs from Mycenaean and Geometric sites at Porto Rafti and Anavyssos.

Other sites in the vicinity

Was there anything left of those sites? I opened my 'bible', Robin Barber's *A Guide to Rural Attika* (1999). "The huge Perati prehistoric cemetery of chamber tombs" at Porto Rafti sounded promising but his directions led us onto the rocky coast below the chic Apollonia millionaires' compound instead. Chats with most passersby revealed disbelief that any

Vravrona: Artemis's shrine

such thing existed but eventually someone appeared who led us right to it. Even standing on the spot, however, we would never have guessed that the rubble-filled, overgrown gully above and just beyond Apollonia could have yielded anything of note. A spry and friendly grandfather accompanied by three-year-old Vassilis took us on a little tour, claiming that the graves were plundered by Italians in 1957, which sounded improbable given the date. In any case, they look more like foxholes than anything ancient.

Unusually for a once sacred spot, the setting has lost any semblance of mystery or romance. Nevertheless, it does have a wonderful view of the large enclosed bay of Porto Rafti. And on the summit of the pyramid-shaped islet at its mouth, we could just detect the blip or nipple that gave the port its name. For this is no mere protruberance but rather a monumental Roman statue of a seated woman, though nick-named the Tailor (*Raftis*) not Seamstress, thought to represent Oikoumene (the civilized world).

Barber describes other ancient settlements and cemeteries around the harbor, and a more lively imagination than mine might be able to envisage it filled with triremes loaded with obsidian and amphoras, not to mention generations of soldiers. No doubt some vestigial walls must lurk amid the rows of apartment blocks, and indeed we followed one of those nice new brown and yellow signs to a small pinewood with a few stones purporting to be the foundations of a 5th century Christian basilica and a Roman bath complex pocked with brick-lined cavities, which looked more like graves than hypocausts. We decided it was time for lunch.

An hour later, replete, I was still unsatisfied. I had an urge to go back to Vravrona, not to the site but to a large fenced area not far from it, which guards another early basilica. High stone walls and marble columns poked through the underbrush; surely there must be a gap in that metal grid. Keeping to the edge of a plowed field, I struggled up the hill and around the enclosure. My instincts proved right – I have rarely seen a (state-erected) fence in Greece that did not have a hole – so I slithered in. The form of the basilica was intact and impressive: three aisles, three apses, "Ionic" colonnades, red marble bases, even a baptistery complete with pool. It was built in the 6th century to 'purify' the district from the 'pollution' emitted by the pagan shrine.

Even so, Artemis would not be displeased. There were signs that badgers had been burrowing and around the corner, near the museum, a group of people have adopted the hill and replanted it with 4,000 trees and shrubs. Small recompense for view of the destruction being perpetrated further north, it nevertheless gives me hope that this particular corner of the Mesogeia may be spared. ◎

How to get there
Convenient brown and yellow signs for Vravrona start just before Markopoulo, but are misleadingly placed alongside a dirt track, rubble dump or modern church. Ancient Brauron is actually about 8 kilometers to the northeast of Markopoulo. The site and museum are open Thurs-Sun, 8:30 am to 3 pm.

Where to eat
Porto Rafti's tavernas are much more in evidence than its antiquities. There are literally dozens of them along its shores, some pleasantly low-key, old-fashioned establishments with tables right on the sea. My favourite, *Kalos Yialos*, seems always to have *barbounia* (red mullet) fresh from the net, delicious *mezedakia* such as peppery marinated anchovies and grilled octopus and, wonder of wonders, efficient service even on Sunday.

1-2 *The Stoa*
   3 *Girl with rabbit*
   4 *Chapel at Vravrona*

Mining the past in Lavrion

Lavrion, the port on the eastern tip of Attica, must be one of the oldest industrial towns in the world. By the third millennium BC settlers were scrabbling silver from its blood-red earth; the Mycenaeans buried their dead under it; and as early as the 6th century BC until the start of the Christian era, the area was being mined systematically. The mines lay dormant and forgotten until the mid 19th century when an Italian named Serpieri reactivated them, extracting usable minerals from old slag as well as expanding into unexploited lodes. Other industrialists followed him. It might be hard to believe now but around the turn of the last century Lavrion was one of the biggest, most important mineral processing centers in Europe.

One hundred years ago Lavrion was one of the biggest, most important mineral processing centers in Europe.

T oday it seems drowsy and depressed, marred by DEH smokestacks breathing pinkish-brown swirls into the blue sky, derelict industrial buildings and, just about everywhere you look, reddish-black mountains of ugly rubble, waste from the mines. Lavrion has hit a slump, not for the first time; much of its population is out of work, it has become a detention center for Middle Eastern refugees, and the neo-classical buildings from a more prosperous era are either crumbling or undermined by cheap apartment blocks. Despite its spacious, low key *plateia*, one of the most splendid palm groves this side of the Sahara, and the Aegean lapping at its shores, Lavrion is dark and weary, especially compared to shining Sounion down the road, where Byron scratched his name into a column and busloads of tourists are herded on summer evenings to watch the famous sunset. But for all its melancholy atmosphere, Lavrion is far more interesting; much more than a ruined temple and a pretty view, it's a place to spend the day, not just an hour.

I suppose it's only human that while we gasp at the perfection of the Parthenon and marvel at the ideals of Pericles, we almost always forget that the silver mines at Lavrion were a key factor in the Athenian miracle. Without the wealth they produced, Themistocles could not have raised the money to build the fleet that saved Greece from the Persian invasion, Pericles could not have financed the monuments on the Acropolis nor the sheathing of the massive statue of Athena with gold. Nowadays it is common knowledge that the Athenian economy was based on slave labor; if the population of Athens in the 5th century BC was roughly 500,000, as many as 300,000 people may have been slaves. The free citizens – all men – who had the right to debate in the Assembly or spout philosophy in the marketplace numbered only about 40,000. But while laws protected household slaves from abuse and the 'civil servants' earned salaries and lived where they pleased, the 10,000 or so slaves who worked the mines at Lavrion were condemned to short, miserable lives. With but a few days off each year, they would have had to descend shafts ranging from 18 to 122 meters deep, equipped with only an oil lamp, a small ax for hacking the ore and a basket to collect it in. Like moles they groped in the murk for twelve hours at a time, but when they emerged their prospects were not much improved.

In *Daily Life in Greece in the time of Pericles*, Robert Flaceliere writes: "Above ground, the smelting of the ore, which was strongly tainted with sulphur, produced poisonous fumes that destroyed vegetation and gave the surrounding countryside a grimly desolate appearance. It was here that the slaves were lodged, in squalid camp-sites, and without any families – this last provision being imposed to save the extra cost of feeding useless mouths."

Lavrion even had its own slave market at Sounion (Athenians bought and sold their slaves at the Agora), where captives from wars or kidnapping victims were inspected and bargained for. That there were at least two thousand shafts sunk into the Lavreotiki – the hills around Lavrion – shows how intensive the search for silver became, how desperate the need for steady labor. Archaeologists have estimated that some 3,500 tons of the precious metal were hauled out of them, along with 1.4 million tons of lead. The silver was minted into the famous Lavriot owls – the coins of Athens – caches of which have turned up in places as far flung as Tunisia, Spain and even India. The lead was molded into pipes, column joints, weights and seals.

Along with these metals and the cadmium and manganese produced today, the Lavreotiki underworld conceals a phenomenal mineral diversity: pink, yellow and royal blue crystals, flamboyant coral-like branches, and ores of such outlandish shapes and configurations they can mesmerize you for hours. They are exhibited in a museum which no one but a real grouch could complain about visiting. It occupies a quaint two-room building set next to a modern school and an abandoned 19th century factory, and is only open between the hours of 10 am and noon on Wednesday, Saturday and Sunday mornings. Nevertheless, any visit to Lavrion should start here. You won't get 'museum back' and no one in the family will be bored.

Although we may feel uncomfortable at the thought of the suffering silver miners producing the Golden Age, it is both fascinating and moving to prowl around Lavreotiki stumbling over their old workshops. The easiest ones to see are tucked into the slope alongside the 5th century BC theater at Thorikos (turn left towards the power plant rather than right into town). One wonders which came first, the theater or the silver-washing installations. Perhaps there was no incongruity in having work and play situated in such proximity. Right near the theater, so close it could almost be mistaken for a *deus ex machina* tunnel, is the barred entrance to an old mining gallery. It might wind for hundreds of meters under the hill. The roofs of these tunnels were bolstered by wooden supports or columns hewn from the original stone. Damaging these in any way was a crime that carried the death penalty.

Another washing facility can be reached by taking a right off the main road a little before the turn to the theater, but if you're in the mood for exploring, it's more fun to drive up to Agios Konstantinos, the politically correct name for the old district of Kamariza. As you climb above the wonderful palm grove and the pretty old tile roofs of a model workers' housing project of the last century, you'll notice on your right a sprawling wreck of a factory surrounded by high walls. This, the former Compagnie Française des Mines de Lavrion, Serpieri's second venture, is being converted into an ambitious Technological/Cultural Park with EU money and Polytechnic expertise. Planned to contain museums, training facilities, a convention center, housing, and job sites by 2000, it could make Lavrion into an exciting, stimulating place to live. In the meantime, billboards advertise that the project also involves rehabilitating the polluted earth around it. For the moment, it looks as if they've simply bulldozed a hillside and dumped the sludge across the road. I called the office at the Polytechnic to inquire, but only got a student who informed me that a sit-in was in progress.

As you near Agios Konstantinos, follow the signs for Agia Triada, a church near one of the largest, most impressive silver-processing workshops. Up here you could take any one of the dirt roads that squirrel 'round these hills and stumble upon old mine shafts, caves, rubble piles and washing areas. Ironically, the forest fires that periodically sear the region have laid bare dozens of sites that were concealed for centuries,

Mining
the past
in Lavrion

You could take any one of the dirt roads that squirrel 'round these hills and stumble upon old mine shafts, caves, rubble piles and washing areas.

delighting archaeologists if enraging ecologists. But the site near Agia Triada is still wooded and, in its way, idyllic. Huge cisterns, still watertight after 2,500 years, fed an intricate system of basins, channels and sedimentation tanks that resemble a giant game of Go. Here the precious metal would be washed repeatedly to separate it from the worthless earth and other stones that accompanied it. At a later stage it would be fed into kilns, smelted and refined; a series of kilns can be seen near the Olympic Yachts factory on the coast, where curious balls of once molten rock litter the ground.

Sadly, exploration of this promising part of Lavreotiki has to be curtailed. High barbed wire fences cordon off a huge expanse of the area and, for once, these fences have no holes. They protect a big arms factory from snoopers. Frustrating, because they surely hide some interesting workshops. But there is consolation to be had. At Sfyrla, on the other side of Agios Konstantinos, past the intriguing machinery of yet another disused factory, there is a wonderful taverna. Not only is the food delectable, the red or white barrel wine eminently drinkable, the fire roaring on a cold day, the taverna is also a mini museum. If you missed the mineral museum in Lavrion, there are stones enough here as well as some marvelous vintage photos of factory workers and plants to give some inkling of the turn of the century boom.

Lavrion – where the slaves mutinied and ran amok after the Spartans occupied Attica in the Peloponnesian War, where workers staged strikes in 1896, 1929 and 1964 so severe the army was called in break them – is a living history book . Every ruin in this area, ancient or modern, speaks of the tension between employer and employee, between the exploiters and the exploited. Maybe that's why the atmosphere is so heavy; it's not a pretty story and there are no myths to lull us into pretending that it happened too long ago to matter. ○

How to get there

Take the Attiki Odos as far as the Markopoulo exit and follow the signs for Lavrion. The town is 54 km from Athens.

Where to eat

Sfyrla, at Agios Konstantinos (signposted), has been serving up wonderful *mezedes* and grilled meats at reasonable prices since 1948. Open every day but Monday, tel. 22920 22374-5.

Note

This article was written in November 1997. When I returned to have another look in the spring of 2003, I found a bustling Lavrion that looked far brighter. More neoclassical buildings had been tastefully restored, the port was being enlarged, there were trendy looking cafés and tavernas near the waterfront. The Industrial Park had made substantial progress, but forest fires had stripped even some of the new saplings that had begun to turn the hills green again. The expanded port should give a boost to the town, but at present the only ferry using it is the one to nearby Kea.

1 *Old factory, new park*
2 *Silver-washing facility*
3 *Ancient theater*
4 *Neoclassical house*
5 *Part of Lavrion's palm grove*

Zoo story:

the Attica Zoological Park

Airplanes are not the only wings fluttering over Spata. Since May of 2000 the village has been home to the third largest bird collection in the world. With over two thousand birds from 320 species, the Attica Zoological Park is a totally unexpected yet wonderful addition to this changing area. For centuries surrounded by vineyards and olive groves with a smattering of medieval churches, the countryside around Spata has been ravaged in the past decade by bulldozers, cranes and other heavy machinery laying runways for the new Athens airport and the ambitious Attica Highway leading to it. But once you're on zoo property, there's no hint of development frenzy. You enter another world.

A well-run zoo is like an ark, preserving species until the human race grows up enough for us all to live together.

S tanding sentinel at the entrance is Katie, an eagle owl as tall as a toddler, from South Africa. When she's not on duty, she either rides around on a keeper's arm or is let free to spread her wings within a large enclosed area. Her round eyes betray no fear for she was born in captivity, in the Eagle Heights Park for birds of prey in the UK, and is used to an audience.

Past the ticket office, the air pulsates with bird noises, surprisingly unmusical. Twitters, squawks, cheeps, screeches, caws, hoots, growls, mews and only the occasional trill. I'd need a tape recorder to do it justice. Down the middle of this 55,000 square meter expanse are ponds with ducks, geese, flamingos, pelicans and other water birds at either end, while the center is occupied by a couple of hangar-like buildings for the tropical birds and three vast aviaries. Enter these enclosures and you stroll amidst birds from Africa, Asia and the Americas in a facsimile of their natural habitat, with no fences separating you from them. Poor Tippi Hedren (remember Hitchcock's "The Birds"?) would not be happy here, but for those not afflicted with ornithophobia it's a thrilling experience.

To the left of the entrance stand spacious cages with dozens of members of the parrot family. Sporting their riotous colors and raucous voices, they hang from the wire roofs by their toes or preen each other's feathers. The lovebirds, true to form, perch on their branches in twos. Each aviary bears informative labels in Greek and in English with names, a geographic distribution map, diet, habitat and prevalence, from common to rare and headed for extinction.

Opposite the parrots are the flightless birds – emus, ostriches, peacocks, rheas, penguins, and other large birds like hornbills and cranes, plus the zoo's few mammals – a lynx, wallabies, Muntjac deer and peccaries. Other large cages, all spotlessly clean, show off the zoo's many species of birds of prey and night birds, while one of the attractive Corfu-pink buildings houses dozing snakes and lizards in cozy stone-lined cubicles.

If you're thinking that there's no such thing as a good zoo, that no wild animal should be imprisoned in a cage, think again. A well-run zoo is like an ark, preserving species until the human race grows up enough for us all to live together. We have seed banks to collect varieties of fruits and vegetables that are rapidly going out of style. Isn't it even more important to keep alive the birds, reptiles and

mammals that provide our planet with such wonderful diversity?

Jean-Jacques Lesueur, the zoo's founder and director, believes the answer is a resounding yes. He is also convinced that the presence of such a place in Greece, whose reputation for the care and treatment of both wild and domestic animals is not untarnished, will not only enhance the country's image abroad but will set an example for people here. The Attica Zoological Park belongs to the European Association of Zoos and Aquariums (EAZA) which has established humane standards for keeping animals in captivity. These include meticulous regulations concerning diet and health, education of visitors, and breeding programs for endangered species. Leaving nothing to chance, the care of bears alone merits a 22 page document.

"Membership in EAZA gives us access to animals from other zoos we wouldn't have otherwise," says Mr. Lesueur. "And of course everything is regulated by the CITES convention [on International Trade of Endangered Species], which requires a declaration of the origin of all products of nature that move between countries. In fact, hardly any of the birds and animals here have been lifted from their natural habitat. They are mostly surplus from other zoos or bred for the purpose and couldn't survive in the wild even if we let them go free."

Born in Paris in 1944, Lesueur has been a passionate birder since the age of three. "My grandfather started sending me books about birds before I could read, and growing up in Casablanca, where my father had a bottling plant, I always had birds and animals. But I kept my birds in aviaries, never in small cages."

As he says this, he jumps up from his desk and pulls down a tiny cage from a shelf in his office. "Look at these prisons, they're horrible. I've known people to keep as many as six birds in one of these and then hang them from the ceiling where they're exposed on four sides. I'm going to make a collection of these cages into an exhibit on how not to treat a bird."

Creating a zoo might seem like an unusual venture for a foreigner whose career started in 1969 as a representative of a British head-hunting firm in Greece, where he and his family had spent summers since 1955. When they wanted to transfer Lesueur to Australia, he refused to budge and set up his own company before eventually moving on to importing and publishing such magazines as *Elle, Playboy* and a host of others. But Lesueur plays down his feat. "Greece doesn't have a proper zoo, I love birds, so I just got to work."

And in record time, too. He leased the property, acquired a building permit in June 1999 and opened in May of the following year. "I designed the zoo myself, improvising as we went along. There was a lot of trial and error but there's no such thing as a specialist in zoo design and so I had to become one, deciding how to arrange the open areas, build the enclosures and aviaries, plan the landscaping."

As for the financing, much of it has been covered by sponsors. So far, fifteen companies, as disparate as Evga, Kodak, Friskies and Trident, have given the zoo support, adopting exhibits in exchange for exclusive rights to sales in its shop and cafeteria. But what about Famous Grouse? "Oh," says Lesueur, "it was a natural thing for them to do. They already have a bird protection program in South Africa, so they're onto ecology."

Not content with supervising the 16-18 staff members who look after the birds, grounds and facilities, Lesueur is thinking of adding more animals – "monkeys, big cats, and others because the public keeps asking for them." But nobody need fear that they will suffer the fate of the pathetic lion that once languished in the National Gardens near Syntagma. Like those already in residence at the Attica Zoological Park, they will be given all the food and vitamins they require in clean, well-aired quarters. Meanwhile, take your children out to the zoo and see for yourselves. Your misgivings about Greek zoos might just be for the birds! ○

The Attica Zoological Park is open every day all year long, from 10 am to 5 pm (October-April) and 9 am to 7:30 pm (May-September). It is located on the outskirts of Spata: there are some signs, turn south at the Veropoulos supermarket, take your first left, and then left again at the Spata cemetery. Call 210 6634724-5 for further information. Entrance fee: Adults €9, children 3-12, €7.50, younger children and disabled people free, and special rates for school groups.

Note
The world's other major bird collections are Walsrode near Hamburg, Germany, and the Jurong Bird Park in Singapore.

Katie the eagle owl

30 Day Trips & Weekends

The Peloponnese and Central Greece

Corinth

for love or money

In 1947 Osbert Lancaster wrote, "The Isthmus of Corinth is one of the dreariest stretches of country in Greece." And that was before highways, factories, gas stations and factory-sized cafés obliterated any trace of scenery. As we hurtle by Corinth on the way to Patras or Tripoli, the blur of flat-roofed greyish-white buildings crammed against the Gulf promises nothing worth a detour. The only landmark we might half-glance at is the crenellated rock of the High City, Acrocorinth, but on we rush.

When Corinth was the richest city in Greece, Aphrodite's handmaidens made thousands of sailors and travelling salesmen happy in the name of love.

Thousands of years ago, however, if we happened to look up as we crossed over the isthmus to Pelops' Island, we might have thought we'd seen Pegasus rising from its craggy summit. The hero Bellerophon, a son of Poseidon whose mortal father was King Glaukos of Corinth, found the mythic horse grazing there, a gift from his god-father. With a golden bridle from Athena he managed to tame the winged stallion, and the two frequently flew off the rock in search of monsters to slay.

Some time earlier, Corinthos – any name ending in 'inthos' is pre-Greek – was founded by Bellerophon's grandfather Sisyphus, whose wilyness makes Odysseus look like a boy scout. Albert Camus thought Sisyphus must have been happy in Hades, at least he had a job to do, but the ancients viewed his eternal boulder-pushing as an example of the worst possible fate. Sisyphus lost Zeus's favour when he was strolling on the heights of Acrocorinth one day and just happened to see the father of gods and men flying by with a nymph named Aigina in his embrace. Of course he saw where they landed. From Acrocorinth you can see forever, even now on a clear day. When the nymph's father, Asopos the river god, passed through in search of her, Sisyphus offered to trade his secret for a spring that would never run dry. And so the Gibraltar-like rock received its water source, and Sisyphus – much later – his punishment.

Other myths relate that Acrocorinth initially belonged to Helios, the sun god, who gave it to Aphrodite. Medea had the first temple to her built and centuries later, when Corinth was the richest city in Greece, Aphrodite had a thousand hand-maidens serving her and making many more sailors and travelling salesmen happy in the name of love. There are no traces of Mycenaean occupation on this wonderfully fortified rock, but there are many reminders of later residents. You have to climb up three stretches of loose cobbling and pass through three gates to enter the citadel. The first gate was built by the Turks, the second is part-Frankish with Venetian reinforcements, while the huge blocks in the third are unmistakably ancient Greek. Inside, piles of rubble poking through the yellow mustard and white pear blossom hint at just how densely the place was inhabited from Byzantine through Ottoman times. There are shells of churches with ogival arches and domed mosques with truncated minarets, but not a whiff of perfume nor a marble couch to conjure up the atmosphere of what must have been a vast bordello.

The city proper lay directly below, some distance from the sea and a few kilometers from the modern town, which didn't exist until the 1850s. The ruins, which the American School has been excavating since 1896, are essentially Roman, because General Mummius razed it to the ground in 146 BC, when Corinthians shouted their preference for independence rather than Roman rule. The only building he left standing was the stolid, Doric temple of Apollo, which still has seven columns unbudged by earthquake or invader. He even demolished the South Stoa, the longest colonnade in ancient Greece, and made off with countless statues that now grace Italian museums.

Controlling all traffic over the Isthmus, Corinth was a power for at least three centuries before Athens started to look westward. Inveterate traders, Corinthians founded colonies in Sicily and Corfu, dispatched ships loaded with scented oils and fine pottery to Spain, the Black Sea, Egypt and Phoenicia, and may have invented the trireme. The city-state's most famous ruler, Periander, was one of the Seven Sages and built the *diolkos* or paved slipway by which boats could be dragged across the Isthmus from the Saronic to Corinthian Gulf and vice versa. But by the mid 5th century BC being midway between Sparta and Athens was less than desirable, and the city was squashed by both belligerents. Nevertheless, trade continued and so must have debauchery, because that's what is left of Corinth's reputation.

Still, it must have been fun. You could watch gladiators fighting lions in the odeon, mock sea-battles raging in the theater, and all those beautiful women added spice to every event. When Pausanias was writing his travelogue in the late 2nd century AD, among the first things he noticed was a statue, not of a deity or distinguished statesman, but of the most famous courtesan, Lais, which shows where Corinthian priorities really lay. Another landmark was Glauke's fountain, which is the first monument we see today even before entering the site. Glauke threw herself into its waters after donning the poisoned robe Medea had sent as a wedding gift to spite her erstwhile lover Jason, but nothing could stop its burning. The Corinthians thereupon stoned Medea's children, who had brought the robe, and subsequently erected a shrine to them nearby in penance, though that has disappeared. (It seems Euripides bent the myth to forge a better tragedy.) The fountain today looks like a misshapen cube and it's hard to see where the water would have been. A much finer example of fountain art is the Roman Peirene, a still vigorous spring disguised by arches, pools and painted grottoes that was donated by Herod Atticus, whose largesse benefited so many Greek towns.

The Corinth forum is a spacious area, below Apollo's temple and above the Peirene fountain, bounded to the north, west and south by the

Corinth:
for love
or money

St. Paul spent
eighteen months
in Corinth, where
he was inspired
to write the famous
line, "It is better
to marry than
to burn."

remains of arcades that housed dozens of shops, mainly taverns, judging from the incredible amount of drinking vessels found in their wells and rubble. Most of them were two stories high and might have been used as hostels; a few of their vaulted roofs are still in place. Drains and pipes crisscross the site; the Romans were nothing if not excellent plumbers. Here and there stand weathered statues with pleated togas and column capitals, the majority with the acanthus leaves that were the city's trademark. And smack dab in the middle of the forum is the Bema, a large rostrum, where it is thought the Roman consul Gallio told the amassed crowds that he had no intention of prosecuting St. Paul as some of the Jewish population were begging him to do.

St. Paul spent eighteen months in Corinth, trying to convert the townspeople to Christianity. After his case was dismissed, he left for Ephesus and from there wrote his two famous *Letters to the Corinthians*, the first of which has more memorable quotes than the rest of his Epistles combined. It is ironic that his famous passage on love (mistranslated "charity" in the King James version) and his caution, "It is better to marry than to burn," should have been addressed to them. For with a thousand courtesans in residence there is no indication that anyone was burning with frustration. Instead, judging from the number of genitals among the terra-cotta votive offerings on display in the museum, and especially in the locked room with finds from the Asklepion, they may have been itching with venereal disease. Poor Paul really had his work cut out for him. ○

Modern Corinth, which has emerged from the rubble of many earthquakes, is not really to blame for its drab demeanor. Besides a sea breeze and a green park, it has one great asset: its folklore museum near the waterfront. Costumes from all over Greece, in mint condition, are on display along with a stuffed yoke of oxen pulling a plow, a straw shepherd's hut, and a country kitchen. The exquisite fabrics, embroidery and accessories are in their way a powerful reminder of the very human glory that used to be Greece, and not so long ago.

How to get there
Modern Corinth is about 1 hour's drive or bus ride from Athens, the ancient site is 5.5 km further west and can be reached by frequent bus from Corinth. For Acrocorinth, you'll have to have your own car or strong legs. The ancient city is open daily from 8 am to 7 pm every day. Acrocorinth has the same hours but is closed on Tuesday.

Where to eat
Though there are several eateries in Ancient Corinth, none is worth a recommendation. I suggest you picnic either inside the citadel or in the grassy theater below the site proper. *Theodorakis' Taverna* near the folklore museum in Corinth proper is reported to have good, fresh fish.

1 *Peirene Fountain*
2,4 *Temple of Apollo*
3 *Acrocorinth*

Dionysian Nemea

Picture this: After years of marriage a royal couple finally manage to have a child, a bouncing baby boy, whom they name Opheltes. So anxious are they to assure his safe progress to manhood, they consult the oracle at Delphi, which utters a rather sound piece of advice: "keep him off the ground until he can walk." In a country crawling with scorpions, snakes and centipedes, this makes sense. Like any true aristocrats, they leave the precious infant in the custody of a nanny, herself a princess from Limnos, a victim of the "white slave trade" of the day.

Ancient Nemea was a fairgrounds where athletes, referees, and hawkers gathered every two years in search of glory, entertainment and an extra drachma.

Meanwhile, trouble is brewing further north in Thebes, where Polyneices and Eteocles, the sons of Oedipus, are squabbling over the throne, and seven generals led by King Adrastos of Argos are marching up to support Polyneices, who married one of Adrastos's daughters. Nemea is not even a day's stroll from Argos, but they arrive in the fertile valley, parched with thirst, for Dionysos (who comes from Thebes, too, in this version of the story) has drained all the rivers. "Let them drink wine, let's have an orgy instead of a war," is his answer to the problem. Arriving in Nemea, the Seven happen upon Opheltes with his nanny. Flustered by the presence of so many impatient and imperious generals, she leads them to a spring Dionysos has overlooked, leaving – oh perfidious female ever distracted by a masculine presence – the baby on a clump of wild celery. Just for an instant, mind you, but long enough for a viper to slither out and poison him, confirming Belloc's adage, "Never leave the hand of nurse, for fear of finding something worse."

The generals are mortified – what a hideous omen – and hoping to propitiate the gods, they hold funeral games in Opheltes' honor. The gods are not mollified, the Theban expedition ends in disaster, but in 573 BC (about seven centuries later), this event becomes the precedent for initiating the panhellenic Nemean Games, where the winners were awarded a crown of celery and a lifetime of free meals in their hometown tavernas.

So many stories whisper through the ruins of ancient Nemea that this site and others in the vicinity become much more than lichen-spattered foundations and column drums in a stunning setting. Here, about thirty minutes' drive from the Corinth Canal, is where Hercules accomplished his first labor and strangled the dreaded lion. Not far away at Tenea the young Oedipus tended sheep, unaware of his Freudian destiny. But mostly Nemea was a fairgrounds, where athletes, referees, spectators and hawkers gathered every two years in search of glory, entertainment and an extra drachma. It never had a permanent population – at least not until the early Byzantine era – so the cases in the museum are full of coins, offerings and temple bits and pieces rather than cooking pots. There is no great work of art among the exhibits either, anything of value having long since been ransacked.

One halcyon Saturday in January we decided to revisit Nemea, taking the old road to Argos one way and returning to Athens via the new Tripoli highway. We left the old road at the turn for Ancient Kleonai. Homer referred to it as "well-built," but there's nothing left to prove this except for some forlorn remnants of "Hercules' Temple" (signposted but not really worth the detour) lying forgotten in a tangle of withered vines. We followed the signs to Ancient Nemea and "Archaeological Place" over winding roads through gentle hills whose every inch is given over to the cultivation of either grape or olive, and left the car in the "University of California Plaza" parking lot.

The excavations at Nemea have been the responsibility of the American School of Classical Studies since 1924, but it was not until the University of California started work in the early 70s that Nemea really began to be studied systematically. In addition, the university raised money from hundreds of private American citizens, bought land, trained workers, built a museum and uncovered the stadium, which is now in such impeccable condition that a version of the games was re-enacted there in 1996 and in 2000 and will be again in 2004.

Although the day was bright and sunny, the museum was chilly, informative rather than spectacular but an essential first stop towards understanding the past. Some of the coins retrieved from careless visitors fill the first showcases. Usually, these little darkened scraps of metal leave me completely indifferent, but some of them were magnified on the wall, making it possible to admire the workmanship in the Athenian owl, Corinthian Pegasus and turtle of Aigina. Kleonai's symbol was a head of Hercules capped with the skin of the Nemean lion and on the reverse side a crown of celery, while that of Argos was especially apt: a wolf's head with bared teeth. Kleonai and Argos were archrivals for control of the games, and they were actually held in Argos for far longer than in Nemea itself. Hanging beside the coin display is a large map showing the provenance of the coins and the origin of the spectators and athletes. People traveled from Sicily, Cyprus and all over Asia Minor as well as the far reaches of the Greek mainland to attend the games.

Such travel was possible because of the ban on warfare for several weeks before, during and after all four major panhellenic athletic tournaments: the Pythian games at Delphi and the Olympics held every four years and the Isthmian and Nemean games held every two. Their scheduling according to the solar

calendar meant that summers were a time of peace in Greece – at least in theory.

But despite the tranquil aura hovering over the ruins, Nemea had its share of violence. At the end of the first section of path a medieval skeleton lies exposed behind a plexiglass window. It belonged to a sixty-year-old woman, mother of at least two children and suffering from osteoporosis and arteriosclerosis. She was a Christian and we may presume that she died a natural death. On the other hand, the poor Byzantine farming community that lived here during the 5th and 6th century was routed (if not murdered) by Slavs, who poured into the Peloponnese after breaching Justinian's walls near the Isthmus. The skeleton of the very last Christian to survive is also preserved. It was found in the tunnel to the stadium, where the doomed man had scratched his name, a poignant message to posterity.

The foundations of the Christian basilica can only just be traced if you walk up the steps near the grave, but this area is a hodgepodge of confusing stones because the church was built on top of the 4th century BC *xenon* or hotel where some of the athletes and their trainers stayed during the games. The Christian practice of digging graves, and irrigation channels for their vegetable patches, damaged the ancient evidence much more drastically than centuries of plundering for construction materials.

Nevertheless, neither the muddle, nor the occasional puddle – for the springs that fed the baths are no longer subject to Dionysos's drought – detract at all from the attractiveness of the site. Protected by a shed, the large bath complex is nearly intact, the sacred grove of cypresses replanted by the Americans recaptures some of the original atmosphere, and the scattered slices of Zeus's columns have been reordered, ready to be set back in place one of these days. (See Note.)

Dionysian Nemea

A visit to the 4th century BC stadium is even more evocative, thanks to a booklet sold at the museum with drawings by Manolis Korres and text by Stephen G. Miller, director of the digs. The stadium lies a short walk from the museum below a hill where the Lion had its lair. It is preceded by a mossy square enclosure prosaically described as the "locker room," where the young men would strip, oil their bodies and, no doubt, tease and strut. Dozens of graffiti are scratched on the walls of the tunnel leading from this courtyard into the stadium, a testimony to male vanity. The most famous says "Akrotatos is beautiful," while below someone has wryly retorted, "to the guy who wrote it," in other words, Akrotatos himself.

Aided by the booklet, we tried to conjure up the scene: the cheering/heckling crowds (possibly as many as 40,000 people, all men, presumably because all the athletes were nude), the judges in their stand by the tunnel, the blistering sun, the thirsty scooping up water from the channel that circles the track, and the glistening boys, "beardless youths" or young men lined up, toes curled over the starting block. Besides the races of various lengths and the pentathlon, there were the contact sports: wrestling, boxing and the brutal pankration, where only

In the Nemea of today Dionysos still reigns supreme. The district is one of Greece's biggest producers of red wine.

gouging and biting were forbidden and the loser could well end up dead. Horse races, with both chariots and jockeys, also took place but at the as yet undiscovered hippodrome. These were the only events in which women could participate, from a distance, as owners. There were no music, drama or poetry competitions. Nero did not play his violin here as he did at Olympia. In fact, long before the Romans were competing, the games had been moved for the last time to Argos (in the 3rd century BC).

Elsewhere in Nemea Dionysos still reigns supreme. The district is one of Greece's biggest producers of red wine, from the local *agiorgitiko* grape or cabernet sauvignon. Local wineries line the roads but don't invite drop-in tastings *à la manière* de Bordeaux or Bourgogne, alas. If you're tempted to buy, go to a bona fide vineyard and not one of the stands purveying Lion's Blood or Hercules' something or other.

Peckish by now and without a picnic, we were not enticed by any of the sorry looking eateries in the modern village of Nemea, whose mishmosh of architectural styles and cluttered streets is as dreary as the countryside is beautiful. We discussed it over mounds of fresh *kalamarakia* at Isthmia in the taverna alongside the canal, until distracted by the flash of a kingfisher's emerald wings across the water. ⭘

Travel tips

The Peloponnesian village and site of Nemea is 39 km from the Corinth Canal via the old road to Mycenae and Argos and 27 km via the new road to Tripoli. It is a wonderful day-trip destination from Athens or it can be explored as part of a longer itinerary around the Argolid. The site/museum and the stadium are open daily except Mondays from 9 am to 3 pm. Admission to the museum costs €3; an extra €1 euro will get you access to the stadium.

Where to eat

If you don't want to drive as far as Isthmia, there is a *psistaria* on the old road not too far from Nemea, and there are eateries in Nemea itself, but nothing worth a recommendation.

Note

This article appeared in January 1999. Since then a fourth column has been added to the temple of Zeus, and archaeologist-in-charge Stephen Miller plans to re-erect more. While making the site more complete for present-day visitors, it is nonetheless controversial. During the 19th century, countless European lovers of antiquity passed by Nemea and, lacking cameras, sketched or painted the famous temple. Many of these paintings, together with written descriptions from that era, are on display in the antechamber of the museum.

1   *Temple of Zeus*
2   *Entrance to Stadium*
3   *The locker room*
4   *Temple of Zeus, detail*

Ziria:
Switzerland in the Peloponnese

"Are you sure this is a good idea?" We looked at each other in horror and dismay. The once lush hills above the gulf of Corinth have been devastated by summer fires. Charred pine and cypress skeletons tilt at crazy angles, baring ribbed flanks so steep and eroded it will be a miracle if any plant takes root here again. Blackened trunks mock the poppies blazing at their feet. For kilometers on end there's not a green leaf in sight. The only consolation is the explosion of roses outside every roadside home, no matter how humble.

Ziria is Hermes' mountain.

B ut as we climb higher and higher above the coast, vineyards and olive groves replace the spectral grimness. They in turn give way to planetrees, pines and walnut trees as we enter Mesaia Trikala, the second of three villages in the region. We've booked rooms in Ano Trikala, three minutes further away, but one glimpse of the stained cement walls and rusty balconies sends us into reverse mode without a second thought. Our guidebook had warned the four provincial pensions in the area lacked charm, so we were prepared to rough it, but there are limits. Luckily, the middle village is changing, and the smart stone hotel I'd noticed the first time around could not be more welcome or welcoming. Its thirty-something owner, Vasilis Boultas, has renounced Los Angeles madness for the beauty of rural Greece.

He tells us a mini ski resort is planned for Ziria. Is that why new hotels are going up, or have the locals been shamed into improving conditions for visitors by the authors of *Unexplored Peloponnese*? They take the Trikalans to task for neglecting their heritage of old churches and mansions, failing to promote their traditional products and leaving their mountain trails unmapped and unsigned.

And yet the next morning the hotel supplies a detailed map-brochure; we find prominent signposts at intervals along the mountain for the main walks; and several dirt tracks have been graded and widened into decent roads. It is true that the church where St. Gerasimos first preached would have any pilgrim in tears at the squalor; that the three-story stone mansion erected by the distinguished Byzantine Notaras family is collapsing; and that pretty houses can be counted on one hand. But once outside the village boundaries and alone with nature, all we care about is the magnificent mountain.

Ziria is a Slavic word meaning 'acorn', though it's hard to see the resemblance. Kyllini, its other name, comes from the ancient Greek *kyllos* or cavity. It is a massive range, with eight peaks higher than 2000 meters, separated into Mikri and Megali Ziria by that cavity, a wide plateau. Some of the higher peaks are still streaked with snow. The plateau and Refuge A are our first destination and we arrive to find truck-loads of sheep spilling out onto a pasture spangled with yellow and white flowers. Newly shorn, the sheep are bellowing their outrage at several different frequencies. The refuge is inhospitably triple-locked but below it a brand-new observation pavilion stands at the spot where three trails start: to the ridge, down the Flamouritsa gorge and to Hermes' Cave. The bald peaks look too much of a slog, the way to the gorge dauntingly steep, so we take the gentle, cone-strewn path towards the cave. Thick firs, all sporting shamrock-green new growth, Mediterranean pines with yellow 'candles' at the tips of their branches, and towering black pines with lopsided branches cover every inch of mountainside with forest, below, above and across the way.

Ziria is Hermes' mountain. His first act after emerging from the cave where he was born was to fash-ion a lyre out of a tortoise shell and some strands of sheep gut (commemorated in the local place-name Helidorea). His third act was to give it to Apollo, to make up for his second, stealing the older god's cat-tle. He also invented the pipes played by his son Pan in settings like this.

Realizing that we have no torch for spelunkering, we turn back only to find that the plateau has been invaded by two tour buses. Their passengers too seem to be grazing; bottoms up, plastic bags and penknives in hand, these are Athenians browzing for *horta* (wild greens). My son says, "*I trella paei sta vouna*" (madness takes to the mountains), altering a popular Greek saying which says the opposite.

Back in the car, our wanderings take us closer to the grey summit, past ravishing flowers – familiar and unknown, including several clumps of golden tulips – and, most unexpected, an Italian camper van. The word '*Limni*', painted in red on a breeze-block, points the way to Lake Dasiou, picturesque but alarmingly shallow for this time of year. In the other direction, an equally promising road looks as though it will take us around the mountain, but halfway there it dwindles into a mud track. A shepherd lad on an antique Honda considers our low-slung car dubiously. "Slowly, slowly, you might get there, but it will break your head."

Switzerland in the Peloponnese

Retracing our steps is no hardship in such surroundings, with a new flower or photo-op at every turn, and back we go to the Trikalas. There are three villages, Kato, Mesaia and Ano (Lower, Middle and Upper) and the name denotes their three good things (*tria kala*): abundant water, fertile soil and a healthy climate. Athenians have discovered them as retreats in autumn and winter, for rambles and cross country skiing. The projected ski slopes have been promised for the past twenty years and if ever completed will consist of just two beginners' lifts.

The next day we plunge further into the Switzerland of Greece, as some brochures call it: from Trikala over to Karya, which is one big walnut orchard, past landscape that looks more like Colorado than Switzerland, with giant reddish bluffs bursting from the fir forests; alongside a river (more bed for plane-trees than rushing water course); and through a series of attractive villages – Goura, Mesino, Steno – better kept than the Trikalas. Below us is the Feneos valley, rimmed on one side by Ziria, on the other by Helmos. Obviously an alluvial plain in some distant age – as we cross, it feels as though we are half under water, a sea of wheat rippling at window level.

The name 'Trikala' denotes the region's three good things: abundant water, fertile soil and a healthy climate.

We are ostensibly following signs to Archaia Feneos, though signs are all that exist of the ancient city. Archaia Feneos is actually the former village of Kalyvia (or 'shacks') which has attempted to improve its image with a name change. It boasts a small museum that is perpetually closed. But no matter. We have come to see Lake Doxis, which did not exist the last time we were here, at least twenty years ago, camping in the west part of the valley, unable to sleep for the nightingales.

The lake has only been there since 1997. But I recognize the little church; now on an islet, it used to preside over the valley from a round hill and I have an old photo to prove it. Close to shore a white cross from the flooded cemetery pokes through the surface, like Excalibur. Trees grow at the edge of the water, which sends back their reflection in as many hues of green as nature possesses. To the north, the red and robin's-egg-blue walls of Agios Georgios monastery sound an incongruous note amidst the dense firs, but nowhere near as loud as the cacophonous carousing of a thousand frogs.

You can even hear them at the monastery, which moved up the hill from the valley in 1693. Not only does it have a spectacular view, it has

Switzerland
of the
Peloponnese

a beguiling otherworldliness and little that is newer than the mid 18th century, when every inch of the church walls was covered with vivid frescoes. Father Gennadios, the abbot, who presides over two other monks, has a rare twinkle as he feeds us spoonfuls of his own exquisite rose-petal jam. "I haven't been to America, but I've been to Australia and Europe and believe me, nothing can compare with what we have here in Greece."

I'm inclined to agree. "Better than Switzerland." Okay, it's not as clean, the roads leave much to be desired, and it's certainly not as well organized but if it were, Greece might be more like Florida, "for the newly wed and the nearly dead," as an old friend is wont to say. Nevertheless, after a superb lunch, as we drive slowly through more breath-taking scenery around Kastania and then down to Lake Stymphalia's reedy banks, I can't keep the late great Douglas Adams out of my mind. Taking the road back to Kiato and the coast is a sobering jolt back to the reality of summer infernos, fast approaching. The title of one of Adams's last books sounds like a portent: *Last Chance to See?* I hope not, but take my advice and head for Ziria before it's too late. **O**

How to get there

We took the National Road to Xylokastro, 30 km from Corinth, on the north coast of the Peloponnese, and then drove another 30 km up into the mountains to Trikala. You can also approach the area from Kiato, Stymphalia and Kastania.

Where to stay

There are two charming small hotels in Mesaia Trikala, the *Mysaio* (27430 91141 / 6977431697) and *Helidorea* (27430 91444-5). We stayed at the *Mysaion*, which opened in January 2001 and boasts fireplaces in every room. Owner Vasilis Boultas, who has spent most of his life in Los Angeles, looked after us well. Breakfast and the *Athens News* are included in the price of the room. In the Kastania area, the *Xenia* (27470 61283-5), newly renovated and under private management, would be a good, perhaps the only, choice there; it has the best view of the three.

Where to eat

In Trikala, at the *7 Aderfia* next to Mysaion, where the rabbit *krassato* (in wine sauce) and lamb with home-made noodles were succulent and the wine, both red and white, excellent. Across the street *Ta Tria Platana* is also reputed to be good value, but was closed for repairs. Near Archaia Feneos, on a hillside just above Lake Doxis, *To Koutouki tou Staikou* (27470 61166) could not be a more appealing place to have lunch. There are lots of dishes featuring local cheeses – creamy *saganaki*, pungent *tyrokafteri* – grilled meat, salads, fabulous sausage and a wine pitcher that seemed to have a hole in the bottom it emptied so fast. Staikos is yet another city dweller who has opted for the clean air and relaxed living of these splendid surroundings.

1 *Lake Doxis*
2,5 *Ziria*
3 *Mountain path*
4 *Wild tulip*
6 *View of Ano Trikala*
7 *Lake Doxis, detail*

The Argolid without tourists

Arguably the heartland of Greece, the cradle of civilization from Mycenaean times and even earlier, the Argolid has probably seen more history than any other part of the country, aside from Athens. And even Athens had longer periods of obscurity. Most visitors make the tour of the Argolid's four-star sites – Mycenae, Nafplion and Epidavros – within days of their arrival in Greece, but few people, even long-term residents, take the time to seek out the less famous attractions in the area, which cover the spectrum from neolithic to neoclassical.

A panoply of gods have ruled over Argos.

The Argive Heraion

Just a few kilometers south of Mycenae, lies Hera's most illustrious sanctuary, an open, spacious site laid out on terraces at the foot of a steep hill. As with so many ancient holy spots, it is the setting rather than the ruins themselves that touch us. There is not even a story, no tales of love, deceit and murder, no bloody bathtub to titillate our imagination, but the view alone is "worth the detour" as the Michelin guide would say.

The parking lot was empty, the guard was washing his car, and we climbed the monumental staircase past the foundations of an enormous arcade, a hostel and

a gymnasium. Hera's temple stood on the second terrace, sheltering a gold and ivory statue of the goddess by Polykleitos. Eight meters tall, it was said to be as grand as Pheidias's statue of Zeus at Olympia. In her right hand Hera held a pomegranate, the symbolism of which Pausanias says coyly "is a secret, so I'll leave it out." In her left she clutched a cuckoo, a reference to her wooing by Zeus. Maybe because she was his sister, Zeus was too shy to approach her directly, and so one blustery winter day he took the form of a shivering bird, knowing Hera would take pity on it. Once enfolded in her warm robes, he shed his disguise, but Hera resisted his advances until he promised to marry her. Interestingly, the cuckoo signifies secret love in English legend, too.

Hera was the patroness of Argos. Originally she had been goddess of the heavens, and her union with Zeus represented the coming together or even subordination of goddess worship to the worship of male gods. Some scholars maintain that the tempestuous relationship between Zeus and Hera reflected the uneasy truce between the two systems of belief, while the ancients are said to have viewed their passions as explanation for crazy weather.

Though most of the ruins date from the 5th century BC, worship of the goddess at this site began in Mycenaean times. The first wooden temple occupied the uppermost terrace. At this spot, so open to the skies, the power of Hera's cosmic nature can still be felt. Nothing is left of the temple, which burned to the ground when an elderly priestess fell asleep instead of tending the altar lamps, but the platform, paved with huge slabs, continues to be majestic and it's from here you get that remarkable view. The plain of Argos stretches out to the east, south and west, with grey-green olive groves in the foreground and dark green citrus groves everywhere else, occasionally interrupted by the dazzle of a glazed hothouse roof, as far as the sea. To the west, the citadel of Larissa crowns the pyramidal mountain above Argos, which claims to be the oldest city in Europe.

Argos

Sad to say, age is no guarantee of beauty, and some irreverent travel guides (Greek, not foreign) dare to rank Argos as one of the ugliest cities in Greece. Certainly the outskirts are disastrously congested, dusty and charmless. Even the center of town has little that invites you to linger, though pedestrianized streets, a remodelled main square and a string of upmarket cafés with spanking white umbrellas show that Argos is trying to refurbish its image. Here and there the bright facades of neoclassical buildings stand out against the drab concrete blocks of thirty years ago, reminders that until the mid 1960s Argos was even more attractive than Nafplion. Then newly rich farmers with an urge to modernize called in the bulldozers and demolished blocks and blocks of their past.

The citadel crowns the pyramidal mountain above Argos, which claims to be the oldest city in Europe.

Nevertheless, there are a few reasons to stop for a closer look. First and foremost is the archaeological museum, part of which occupies a neoclassical mansion, just off the main square, that once belonged to Kallergis, a hero in the War of Independence. Its collection of early and late Geometric pottery is superb – one large urn displaying just about every design motif invented by man, from the cross to the swastika, meanders, whorls and squiggles plus the horses for which Argos was renowned. There are statues from the Roman era, splendid Early Christian mosaics of the months and seasons but, most important, a large room devoted to finds from Lerna, the prehistoric site on the coast southwest of Argos. These are surprisingly fine and sophisticated, often decorated with strikingly bold linear patterns. Some come from as far away as Troy, Crete, Milos and Central Greece, evidence of the far-reaching trading contacts of the third millennium BC. A second reason to loiter in Argos would be to wander through its rather

The Argolid
with its
tourists

111

chaotic antiquities. The *Blue Guide* cautions that these are of "specialized interest," and they are difficult to decipher, being a jumble of ancient Greek and Hellenistic buildings remodeled over several centuries by the Romans. But the 4th century BC theater was one of the largest in the ancient world, holding up to 20,000 spectators, eight thousand more than Epidaurus. Carved out of a narrow piece of hillside and encroached upon by pines, it seems strangely cramped now. Next to it rises the ungainly brick remains of a Roman baths complex superimposed upon a large temple of the 1st century AD. Across the street the Agora ruins can be fun to poke around but do not evoke any of the wonderful myths associated with Argos: of Danaos and his 50 daughters, of Zeus ravishing Semele in a shower of golden rain, or of the Seven Kings who marched against Thebes. They do hint at the city's role as a powerful buffer between Athens and Sparta, often caught in the crossfire.

Anyone wishing to explore Argos further will be aided by an illustrated map put out by the municipality and given away at the museum. It will point you to nuggets like the Capodistrias barracks, originally Venetian, or landmark houses designed by Ernst Ziller. But you might be immobilized by fits of giggles at the English translation. The railway station, for example, is a "Neoclassical building of 19th century. It experienced blooming days up to 1960. Central point of trafficking for people & products from and to Athens with other cities of Peloponnese."

Lerna and the Pyramid of Elliniko

If you take what used to be the main road to Tripoli past the ancient ruins, in less than 10 minutes you'll see a sign for Kefalari and the Pyramid of Elliniko. This pyramid is no seventh wonder but still merits a visit for its novelty value. Although the hefty polygonal stones in its construction and its primitive triangular opening look as if they were the work of a junior Cyclops, the building appears to have been a guard house of the 4th century BC. At Kefalari there are also two caves to peer into and a cluster of tavernas under plane trees if you want to linger.

For Lerna, go back to the main road and head south as far as Myli, 10 km from Argos. Lerna conjures up visions of Hercules and his second labor, in which he slew the Hydra, a serpent with nine heads whose terrible 'dragon breath' poisoned any would-be assailant. Cutting off heads was no solution because two sprouted to replace each one. Eventually Hercules defeated the monster with the help of his nephew

Iolaos, who set fire to the forest behind the marsh where the Hydra lurked and was able to burn each head before the new ones could pop up. Once she was dead, Herakles dipped his arrows in her venom and was well equipped to vanquish future foes.

The settlement at Lerna is so old it must predate even the myth, which some analysts view as a symbolic explanation for the taming of the many water sources in the vicinity. The first sign of habitation goes back to the sixth millennium, but what we mainly see are the foundations of a large Early Helladic (mid 3rd millennium) building known as the House of the Tiles, which is not unlike a Moroccan casbah. It is surrounded by storerooms, houses, graves and fortifications of slightly later periods. Now enclosed by a most unromantic shed, the main ruin consists of mud-brick walls with gaps filled by neatly stacked ceramic shingles which once roofed this two-story dwelling. The building burned before it was finished but the area remained populated until Roman times, though never by more than about 800 inhabitants. The guard is sweet but not very instructive, so do pick up a copy of the booklet *Lerna in the Argolid*, by John L. Caskey and E.T. Blackburn, of the American School of Classical Studies, who excavated here in the 1950s. It is sold at the Argos museum and puts life and meaning into the mysterious arrangements of Lerna's stones.

The Argolid
with your
tourists

The Larissa

If the flat, fenced-in settlement of Lerna lacks excitement, the castle of Larissa above Argos certainly makes up for it. From a distance, its crenellated walls, round bastions and square towers proclaim the age of chivalry. You can almost see pennants flapping in the breeze, hear the clattering of armor as Frankish and Venetian knights ride into the enceinte. From closer up, the older stones become visible – carefully hewn masonry of the 5th century BC and polygonal shapes of the 6th – while inside the walls are traces of the original Mycenaean fort. But as you walk through the arched gate, slightly obstructed by the weathered scaffolding of some abandoned restoration effort, a more recent event may quicken your interest.

Picture this: It's July 1822, fifteen months since the Greeks declared their independence from the Ottoman Turks. Mustapha Dramali, the pasha of Drama, has invaded the Peloponnese with 30,000 men. There are only 5,000 armed Greeks to stop him but they are scattered. If he can get through Argos and take Tripoli, the uprising may be snuffed out before it gets started. But first Dramali has to conquer the castle, defended by a mere handful, 700 Greek soldiers, commanded by Dimitris Ypsilantis. He stations his artillery on the Aspis, the lower hill to the east, and opens fire. For ten whole days cannonballs thunder into the old walls but the Greeks stand firm. Meanwhile their compatriots are burning crops and regrouping, so that when Dramali orders his hungry army to retreat, Kolokotronis and his men ambush them at the pass of Dervenakia, according to plan, in one of the first major victories in the War of Independence.

I shudder to think of the bloodshed, the cries and moans of dying men, the pungent smell of gunpowder and worse. And I thank all the panoply of gods who have ruled over Argos that scruffy as some of it may be, today the prevailing smell is of orange blossom, the predominant image orange groves stretching to the horizon. ◯

How to get there

After crossing the Isthmus of Corinth, you can either take the old road that snakes alongside the railway line or the new National Road to Tripoli as far as the exit for Argos. The Heraion lies amidst a tangle of roads northeast of Argos. It is neither near Iraion or Ira but rather beyond Honika, the locals' name for Neo Iraion. There are signs, but if you get lost, a consolation prize is running across one or more of the delightful Byzantine churches in the vicinity. From Argos, all the other sites are clearly marked.

Where to eat

Carnivores will appreciate the reportedly excellent souvlaki served at the roadside grills in Myli or at the tavernas around the square in Kefalari. We enjoyed sole caught that morning, a crisp salad, fried potatoes and a very decent wine at *Faros*, right on the sea at Myli, just past the early 20th century train station and about 100 m east of the main road. Sitting under the trees with the Argolic Gulf at your feet is reason enough to visit Lerna.

Where to stay

Argos has a few modest hotels designed for travelling salesmen, such as the *Mycenae* (tel. 27510 68754) on the main square, but you might be happier in Nafplion at the *Byron* (tel. 27520 22351) or the *King Othon* (tel. 27520 27595), which are more atmospheric and quieter.

1   *The Heraion*
2   *Mosaic, Argos Museum*
3   *Theater and Roman baths*
4,6 *Larissa Castle*
5   *The Pyramid at Elliniko*
7   *View of castle from town*

Ancient Akti:
small bits of a big past

For more years than I care to mention I've been commuting from Athens to Spetses at least once a month. We take the coast road from the Corinth Canal to Palaia Epidavros, never failing to gasp at the stunning glimpses of blue fjords and distant islands through the thick green veil of pine forests and citrus groves. This corniche climbs high above the Gulf of Epidavros and then abruptly shrivels into a winding country lane favored by tractors and Toyota pickups as it slices through hamlets claiming fabulous feta, rocky hills with just as many sheep as stones, unsightly quarries and gardens studded with sea-green cabbages or sun-bright marigolds.

The Greek stones speak, but they don't say much.

The area is absolutely undistinguished: the mountains are low, the olive trees old but not romantic, the villages strung out and unremarkable. So after stopping for a hot, flaky *tiropita* at the baker's in Tracheia, we speed on to Kosta where we hop into a sea taxi for Spetses.

This is a corner of Greece where very little ever happened to warrant mention in a history book. Though so close to the great centers of the Argolid – Mycenae, Argos, Epidavros – the northeast extension of the Peloponnese was even bypassed by myth. Next door, the palace at Tiryns whispers rumors about Hercules, the ghost of young Theseus still lingers in Troezen's glades and streams, but what legends are linked with Ermioni, Porto Heli or Kilada? Even the region's name lacks personality; it was called simply and prosaically, '*Akti*' or 'coast'.

And yet this forgotten peninsula has a story, as I found out while flipping through the pages of Adonis Kyrou's fascinating study, *Sto Stavrodromi tou Argolikou* (On the Crossroads of the Argolic Gulf), in which he traces its past from paleolithic to Roman times. So one weekend, instead of hurtling directly to Spetses, we spent the day wandering in a few of Kyrou's footsteps.

Our first stop was Kilada, which simply means 'valley', a strange name for a port where fishing is the prime activity. Trawlers and kaikis lined the docks, smaller hulls were humped in rows on the beach and everywhere mounds of nets, dyed deep burgundy, soft russet and faded terra-cotta, lay neatly piled. Spread-eagled octopus dangled by the dozens outside fish tavernas where charcoal fires spat and sparked in preparation for Sunday lunch. Nothing in the atmosphere suggested that this was one of Greece's oldest inhabited spots.

On the other side of the bay the blank eye of an enormous cave stared out from a rock-stubbled promontory. Only a few experts have heard of it but the Franchthi cave was home to generations of primitive families from 23,000 to 3000 BC. Stone age implements from an even more remote 40th millennium BC have been found here, the earliest in Greece, but its heyday was the neolithic. Obsidian from Milos also turned up on the floor of this cave, mute but eloquent testimony that its denizens were acquainted with the latest technology and had trade, if not with the distant island itself then surely with 'travelling salesmen' who peddled the precious stone from cave to cave.

Around 3000 BC a catastrophic combination of earthquakes, eruptions and floods devastated the eastern Mediterranean, annihilating most of the population and leaving each civilization with a legacy of cataclysm legends, from Noah to Deucalion. The Franchthi cave was abandoned and never inhabited again, though it was used for the worship of underworld deities in the Classical era. On the headland opposite, a Bronze Age settlement called Mases appeared, but it had none of the glamor of Mycenae; its people had not switched from obsidian to bronze and were still raising goats and sheep rather than horses and cattle. The site slowly sank into an oblivion from which it never emerged. Even today, though shipowner George Livanos transformed the rocky islet at the entrance to the bay into a green haven, it remained outside the public's ken, unlike Spetsopoula and Skorpios, where the notorious antics of his sisters' husbands, Niarchos and Onassis, regularly splashed across the tabloids.

Nowadays, the archaeologists having packed up and moved on, very few people visit the cave, but the three teenaged girls running the port *periptero* told me that you can persuade a fishingboat to take you there in summer (there is no road). They called it Cyclops' sheepfold and interrupted each other, excitedly recalling childhood excursions: "It's a double cavern; with a tiny lake at the bottom; and hundreds of pigeons roost there. They coo so loud you can hardly hear yourself think." They had no notion that, along with the Petralona cave in Halkidiki, it held the key to Greece's earliest societies.

After the Flood, tribe after tribe of nomads from Asia Minor filtered down from Thrace to Thessaly, Attica and the Peloponnese, thirty-two of them in all, becoming Greek in the process. For as Kyrou says, "The Greek soil had the power to make those that conquered it Greek themselves, absorbing and transforming new ideas from the East." Almost as soon as they arrived in the Argolid, the tribes began thrusting outward once more, using the Saronic islands as stepping stones for trade, as well as pasturing their flocks and even smelting their bronze there. They left their mark everywhere – beaches on Spetses full of shards, mysterious rock piles on Hydra and the mainland, a 4,300 year old shipwreck at Dokos – but not much to impress the average nonspecialist.

As the power center shifted from Lerna to Mycenae to Argos, settlements popped up at Ermioni and Porto Heli (ancient Halieis), both boasting sheltered bays. Ermioni was by far the more important, ideally situated for trade with the Aegean. Well before the 6th century BC the Ermionida was producing coveted grain, wine and olive oil (which is still golden and mellow), but its real wealth came

from the humble shellfish that emits the fabulous purple dye that only kings could afford. (A taverna on the waterfront commemorates this in its name, Porfyra.) It also had a special relationship with the goddess Demeter. (Could this be why there are so many pomegranate orchards in the vicinity?) At any rate, they did consider a gorge in the area a shortcut to Hades so, unlike the rest of the Greeks, they never bothered to place an obol in the mouth of their dead to make sure Charon would ferry them across the river Styx.

Pausanias visited the town in the 2nd century AD and told of many splendid monuments, but if you ask a local where the antiquities are, he'll simply wave his hand vaguely and say, "everywhere." And nowhere,

Ancient Akti:
small bits of a big past

because while you will see bits of wall, an entrance to a Mycenean beehive tomb, a Classical well, random blocks of masonry and the huge but columnless base of a mighty temple to Poseidon, the modern town is built upon the ancient one, making excavation impossible. A few years ago, while laying the foundations for a new telephone center, the laborers unearthed a massive lid to a late Roman sarcophagus. Sculpted for a couple, it was never used; the faces on the man and wife were left featureless.

Besides humming with visitors in summer, Ermioni is lively off season too, being the port to which all the fishing boats in the area take their catch for delivery to Athens. So after our pleasant but fruitless prowl round the "archaeological site" on the piney promontory, we consoled ourselves with a platter of *barbounia* (red mullet), greens drenched with exquisite oil, good barrel wine and apples sprinkled with cinnamon and Metaxa at the Akroyiali taverna, and watched the trawlers chug in and out.

At Porto Heli, which was nothing but a marshy lagoon until tourism developers erected a few outsize hotels and several strings of plastic cafés, the past is even less obvious than at Ermioni. At least half the ruins of the town lie under water on the southeast side of the enclosed bay. And many of the rest have never been located, so that all we could find was a small enclosure marked only by the inevitable "No entry" sign and a rusty fence with the predictable large hole in it. Obscured by weeds and neglect, the foundations of a few buildings surround the remains of two enormous storage jars, a couple of wells, a small flight of stairs, and some lined trenches that could have belonged to an olive press. There are terra-cotta pipes for water and a covered drainage channel, indicating a high standard of living, but nothing more.

This was a refugee settlement, offered by Ermioni to civilians from Tiryns when Argos destroyed that town for being on the wrong side in the Peloponnesian War. At its peak it was home to 2,500 people, teetering on the fringes of the rivalry between Athens and Sparta, sometimes witnessing a battle, changing allegiances depending on which city wanted to fortify their port, but mostly just minding their own business. Too bad we cannot resuscitate the place to house the thousands seeking refuge on Greek shores today.

Instead, the area between Ermioni and Porto Heli is fast becoming another Loutsa/Porto Rafti, with the rich vying to build the most desirable villa on the coast and the interior being hacked into tiny plots for the less well-off who also crave a summer house. Give it another hundred years and they will all have turned to rubble, adding another footnote to the long but subdued history of this unsung region. ⊙

How to get there

You can explore Akti as we did, on your way to Spetses, or as a side trip from Epidavros or Nafplion. A new road allows you to approach the Franchthi cave by car.

Where to stay

Ermioni has three adequate hotels, Porto Heli has several large but charmless hotels catering to packaged tours, a couple of humbler ones near the dock – *Flisvos* (27540 51316) and *Porto* (27540 51410) – and the A class *Porto Heli* (27540 51490). Spetses and Nafplion are both well stocked with rooms and hotels in every price range.

Where to eat

Apart from the tavernas mentioned in the text, we have our favorites in Porto Heli and Kilada. There are several restaurants and tavernas, cafés and gelaterias along the dock in Porto Heli. Of those open all year long, we prefer *Archontiko*, at the near end, one street up, for mezedes, and the *Psistaria* opposite it for excellent grilled meat, souvlaki and salads at wonderfully low prices. At Kilada, twin tavernas opposite the main pier are known for their fish. Being owned by brothers, they are both called Megas. Have a look at the display fridges outside and choose the one that has the best catch.

1 *Temple foundations, Ermioni*
2 *Taverna, Kilada*
3 *Roman sarcophagus lid, Ermioni*

From myths to Methana

All I remembered of Troezen was a perfect picnic sometime in the early 70s. We sat on flat rocks at the bottom of a narrow gorge shaded by new greenery. On one side water tumbled by without splashing our sandwiches, on the other a placid pool beguiled us with false promises of a balmy swim. Tentative toe tests told us it was lying. Wine and conversation flowed for hours. We had no thought of Theseus, Hippolytus and Phaedra.

Phaedra was said to have spied on the naked youth from the Temple of Peeping Aphrodite.

To get to our rocks we had crossed the Devil's Bridge which lies above a tower that once belonged to the ancient city walls. Now that I've seen it again I wonder why such a lovely spot should have such a sinister name. The bridge, a natural span between the two sides of a deep slash in the mountainside, could have been made by a benevolent spirit, while the glade formed by the spreading boughs of monumental plane trees would surely have been a preferred trysting place of Aphrodite. I was grateful that, despite these attractions, Trizinia is still so far off the beaten track that no one has yet installed a *kantina* next to the chasm.

The authorities in Trizinia, a pretty village surrounded by traces of the ancient city of Troezen, where Theseus was born, are evidently too sensitive for that. Green and yellow signs point the way to the antiquities and a detailed map of the area is available from a shop in the main square. This pleasant open space overlooks the lemon groves that cover almost all the land between the mountains and Poros and Galatas to the south. Behind its few tavernas and cafés are old houses going back more than two hundred years. One of them had a moment of fame in May 1827 when the fractious rival leaders of the Greek Revolution reconciled their differences long enough to elect Capodistrias president there, where they also drew up a constitution for the as yet unborn republic before they went back to battling the Turks.

A look at the map shows ancient relics scattered throughout the district, from Early Christian churches to Roman graves, but there are no Mycenaean era remains to indicate the palace where Theseus was raised. A boulder, however, has been singled out as the one under which his father, King Aigeus of Athens, hid his sword and sandals for the boy to claim when he was old and strong enough. Troezen had close ties with Athens, having once been its colony, and childless Aigeus had popped in to brainstorm with its king Pittheus over the meaning of the Delphic oracle, which had told him "loosening the neck of the winebag" would solve his problem. Pittheus saw immediately what was in order, relaxed his friend with plenty of wine and dispatched his daughter Aithra to Aigeus's couch (thereby giving new dimensions to the term friendship and acquiring a grandson in the process). As you can imagine, Aigeus was thrilled but cautious (it helps to remember that he was living with Medea!) and left his son Theseus in Troezen to grow up far from Athenian intrigues. Much later, Theseus left his own son, Hippolytus, to do the same, but with far less happy consequences.

Handsome and heroic, Theseus had no use for fidelity. After slaying the Minotaur, he abandoned Ariadne on Naxos and sailed back to Athens with her sister Phaedra, whom he eventually married. But he also found time to sire Hippolytus during a campaign against the Amazons and was so taken with twelve-year-old Helen that he whisked her away from her father long before Paris set eyes on her. Obviously Phaedra had to find some solace. She thought she'd found it in Hippolytus, a beautiful youth who in honor of his Amazon mother had dedicated himself to Artemis and a life of chastity. How tiresome and frustrating. Aphrodite was frustrated, too (and we know how much she liked young men), so she used Phaedra as a vehicle for her own revenge. Hippolytus continued to refuse his stepmother's advances, so fulfilling Shakespeare's observation that "Hell hath no fury like a woman scorned," Phaedra tore her hair and shredded her gown and told Theseus his son had tried to rape her. Gullible Theseus believed her and called upon his patron Poseidon to punish him. The god, whose sanctuary was at nearby Poros, obliged by sending a monster to frighten Hippolytus's horses as he drove along the sea in his chariot and the poor boy was fatally injured.

By some accounts Artemis whisked him off to safety in southern Italy, but the Troezenians were desolate at the loss of the heir to their throne and centuries later continued to mourn him at shrines and games. The main cluster of antiquities includes the foundations of a temple of Hippolytus, the faint outline of his stadium and the appropriately named temple of Aphrodite Kataskopia (or Peeping Aphrodite), where Phaedra was said to have spied on the naked youth as he jogged and wrestled. A church, built on top of it, is fascinating. At one end it has four closed arches, all slightly different and, at the other, the remains of three apses. Dozens of ancient stones are inserted into the walls, columns lie where they fell, and paving blocks show traces of mosaics or sculpted crosses. Mauve flowers sprout from some cracks. The most impressive ruin is a square court which could have been surrounded by water with a spacious sleeping platform on one side. This would have been an Asklepion but it must have seemed like a provincial clinic compared with the big 'health center' or healing sanctuary at nearby Epidaurus.

If you have the map and wish to explore more ruins, you will be rewarded by lovely countryside if not spectacular temples and an exquisite abandoned monastery about five minutes' drive above the village, but we chose to head off for lunch and more unknown territory.

Handsome and
heroic, Theseus had
no use for fidelity.

Methana

Methana evokes foul smells and seedy spa buildings from another
era, which are all you notice when the ferry docks. My husband, who
was dragged there as a small boy one summer so his mother could
benefit from the baths, remembers it as "loaded with melancholia
and desperation." Although the harbor is picturesque from a distance and filled with wintering yachts, closer inspection reveals that
nothing has changed. The prewar hotel where he stayed – the
height of luxury at the time – looks irrevocably boarded up, and the
EOT bathing pavilions are in a state of shameful dilapidation. But
Methana is more than a sad spa; behind it a whole unspoiled peninsula slumbers.

A charming map at the entrance to town pinpoints the land-

From myths
to Methana

marks, all of which are built with the peninsula's reddish-purple volcanic stone, for it boasts an extinct volcano. Heading west brought us to terraced hillsides planted with olive and almond trees and the walls of the seaside ancient acropolis. Beautifully hewn wine-red stones are made even more stunning by the tapestry of orange, yellow and tomato-red lichens woven over them. Very overgrown and barely excavated, the acropolis was built by Ptolemaios II Philadelphos, the Hellenistic king of 3rd century Egypt. On its summit, long curved stones leave no clue as to whether they belonged to a lookout post or a temple.

As we pushed on past the tiny fishing port of Vathy to the volcano, the landscape grew wild, the stones lost their round shapeliness and the road turned into a rutted track. A village, Kaimeni Hora, lived up to its name, pitiful, desolate and almost buried by petrified lava spurs and jagged outcrops. Beyond it the road petered out and we never did make it to the crater; the path that continued on looked half obliterated by fallen rock. Even so, the view was extraordinary, spanning the mountainous coast opposite as far as Palaia Epidavros and, below us, the Krasopanayia, a tiny chapel dedicated by a wine merchant who had vowed to mix his cement with wine should the Virgin save him from a shipwreck.

With more time we would have toured the rest of Methana. Instead we headed back towards Trizinia, intrigued by signs in Hindi. A bilingual shop/café stocks restaurant-size sacks of chillies, dals and spices for the large Indian population who work in the greenhouses and lemon groves. How appropriate that Troezen which had a reputation for hospitality in the past – it offered sanctuary, schools and even a stipend to Athenian women and children during the Persian Wars – should be home to new refugees today. ○

How to get there

You could put your car on the daily (8 am) ferry to either Methana or Poros (smaller car ferries to Galatas on the mainland every 20 minutes), or drive to Tracheia via Nafplion and Ligourio or Isthmia and Palaia Epidavros. About 1500 m before Tracheia the road forks east to Methana and Galatas and south to Kranidi, Porto Heli and Spetses. You can be exploring Methana in less than an hour. To return, you can either take the unpaved mountain road from Trizinia to Rado or Iliokastro and rejoin the Kranidi road or follow the coast to Ermioni, Kosta and Porto Heli. A new direct road from Palaia Epidavros to Methana has been carved out of the steep mountainside but was not yet functioning at the time of publication.

Where to stay

Acceptable no-frills hotels may be found in Galatas, Palaia Epidavro and Ermioni. Try the *Saronis* in Galatas (22980 22356), *Elena Rooms* (27530 41207) or *Marialena* (27530 41138) in Palaia Epidavro and *Ganossis Filoxenia* (27540 31218) in Ermioni. Alternatively, Poros and Spetses have plenty of accommodation in every price range.

Where to eat

Dirlandas (22980 31222) at Kalloni, a few kilometers before the Methana peninsula, is one of the those old-fashioned tavernas right on the water, where the food is delicious, the barrel wine light and and clear, and the service polite and friendly. Three of us had tender lamb chops, perfectly grilled swordfish with a lemony sauce, fried potatoes and a salad for about €30. Not far from either Methana or Trizinia, it is the best place in the area to take a break from sightseeing.

5

1 *Methana harbor*
2-3 *Temple of Aphrodite and church*
4 *Asklepion*
5 *Methana walls*

Underground Elefsina

It's a warm, sunny Saturday at the end of January, not a cloud in the sky though the mountain tops are dusted with snow. We're sitting outside a waterfront ouzeri, lingering over our wine and picking at the last of a platter of shrimps and langoustines, having already slurped up several oysters and clams. Beyond the white sand in front of us, sailboats are lined up alongside cabin cruisers in the marina, and snatches of orange and blue café facades glow through the shrubbery in the square opposite.

I cannot believe this is Elefsina. Gone is the grunge, the pollution. It's so pretty.

The immaculate streets and jetty are paved with designer bricks and flagstones, strategically placed benches have attracted a trio of card-playing oldsters plus a crowd of kibbutzers, and the swings and slides in the two playgrounds are crawling with kids. A tramp steamer, the Volgo Vald from Sankt Petrograd, eases into the port beyond the yachts, and only the pleasing spectacle of the great bay dotted with cargoboats and a smattering of ferries riding high at anchor give the clue that we are not in some trendy new resort.

I cannot believe that this is Elefsina. Gone is the grundge, the pollution. The neoclassical houses have been restored. It's so pretty. "How long has this been going on?" I ask the smiling waiter. "It started about five years ago," he replies. "You should see this in summer, *yinetai hamos* (it's packed)."

The first inkling we'd had that something was afoot in Elefsina was a glimpse of a surreal bar as we drove toward the archaeological site. Painted blue and mustard, the former neoclassical mansion had a bicycle suspended above the front door. On either side of it stood palm trees, stubby ones in a little garden on the right and on the left two royal giants, their fronds like sprays of fireworks. Further down the road, facing the antiquities, virtually every old building had been spruced up and converted into a café or bar. "Elefsina comes even more alive in the evening," said the cheery young woman taking tickets at the site. "Everyone drops by for a coffee or a drink or to listen to music before or after dinner. Mandra and Aspropyrgos have the tavernas, but the rest of the action is here."

No guidebooks I've read, even the latest editions, have ever hinted that Elefsina has more to offer than the bewildering piles of stones and overlapping foundations of the holiest place in the ancient world. Hemmed in by industry, all sense of sanctity destroyed by the dust spewing from the derelict hulk of a cement factory next door, Demeter's shrine has been treated ill by Christians over the past 1500 years. It requires a prodigious imagination to conjure up the processions of priests, initiates and novices winding along the Sacred Way from Athens to take part in the mystic rites. The route is one of the most blighted in Greece. Refineries, factories, and iron mills began eradicating the legendary fields in the Thriassic Plain well before World War II, fields where Demeter herself was supposed to have taught men

2

to cultivate wheat and barley. Not one exists today; the only open space is claimed by the little used military airport. You'd think 'they' could have fenced off a token patch, the way the Americans have designated certain highway islands for the planting of the prairie grasses that have all but vanished from the Great Plains.

But Demeter's cult has never aroused much sympathy amongst Christian leaders. One reason Eleusis, the foremost religious center of the Classical Greeks and Romans, is such a jumble of marble blocks, sculpture fragments, shattered architraves and chopped columns is because the early Church deliberately set out to expunge all trace of its fascination and appeal. As we stand outside the fence trying to make some sense of the bare foundations and mounds of stones, our guide Rick Hartman tells us his theory. "The Church couldn't afford to leave any trace of the Eleusinian Mysteries because they were too similar to its own teachings. Though we don't know exactly what went on there, we do know that the ceremonies promised a life after death – a rebirth, perhaps even reincarnation. If you'd been initiated at least twice, you gained admission not just to the Elysian Fields but to the Isles of the Blessed and joined the ranks of the immortals.

"They also had a kind of Holy Communion, where the initiates drank a decoction of barley flour, mint and water in commemoration of the refreshment given to Demeter by the king and queen of Eleusis. Maybe the revelations and consolation they received during the rites were even more compelling than the promise implicit in Christ's resurrection. The early Church couldn't risk the competition."

And the competition had the advantage of being very well entrenched. Worship of Demeter literally 'Mother Earth', who brought forth life from the soil and governed all creation, and her daughter, who symbolized spring and rebirth, seems to have begun at Eleusis as early as the 15th century BC. After the cult became panhellenic around 760 BC and Eleusis ceased to be separate from Athens, the Athenian rulers invested heavily in successive building campaigns. This means that Mycenaean houses lie under Peisistratid walls and Periclean temple bases, not to mention Roman arches, for the Romans were even more enthusiastic. Keen admirers of Greek monuments, they redesigned the entrance as a copy of the Propylaia on the Acropolis and they kept enlarging the hall where the final rites were held until it could hold ten thousand initiates. This hall was windowless and no one ever revealed what went on inside. Even Pausanias refrained from comment; he'd had a dream "forbid[ding] me to write what lies inside the sanctuary wall, and what the uninitiated are not allowed to see, they obviously ought not to know about."

The Mysteries at Eleusis were overwhelmingly democratic. Any man or woman, free or slave, could take part, provided they could speak Greek (ie, understand the ceremonies) and had "no blood on their hands." But they were forbidden on pain of death to mention any of the proceedings. The miracle is that not one of them ever even hinted at the details over some two thousand years. Scholars have speculated that a pageant may have been performed with Persephone springing miraculously from a crack in Pluto's cave – which yawns darkly to the right of the initiation hall – and that the barley-mint drink might have been fer-

Underground Elefsina

Cicero wrote, "The greatest gift of Athens to mankind and the holiest is the Eleusinian Mysteries."

mented and thus potentially hallucinatory. We'll never know for sure, but the message must have been extremely moving, powerful and personal. As Cicero wrote, "The greatest gift of Athens to mankind and the holiest is the Eleusinian Mysteries."

At any rate, its threat had the Christians scratching crosses into the slabs at the entrance as talismans against the goddess's spell. And of course they immediately built a church on the razed acropolis, but it took many more centuries for superstition to fade. Some thousand years later Albanian farmers, imported by the Turks, settled in Elefsina. The villagers used to pray to a St. Dimitra and brought her gifts of pungent manure and harvest fruits. Rumor had it that her daughter had been carried off by the terrible Turks. Then in the early 19th century, foreigners started poking around the ruins looking for ancient marbles. Sound familiar? A typical England vs. France rivalry ensued, won by Edward Daniel Clarke, a mineralogy professor at Cambridge University, who managed to make off with one of two remarkable Roman karyatids in the image of Demeter. The locals were aghast at the theft of their statue and predicted that any ship carrying it would sink. As indeed it did, but the enterprising English were able to pinpoint the wreck and salvage the contents, while Clarke won renown. The very title of his book, *Greek Marbles brought from the shores of the Euxine, Archipelago and Mediterranean,* will raise the hackles of the anti-Elgin crowd. You can see the karyatid that remained in the Elefsina museum; balancing an elaborate flowerpot-like headdress on her tresses, she still looks capable of inspiring awesome emotions.

One solitary house, newly and nicely restored, still stands inside the archaeological grounds as evidence of that Albanian village. But there are not many Arvanites (as the early Albanians are called) left in Elefsina's one- and two-story houses today. It's a town with few real locals, most of its residents having come from all over Greece and abroad to work in the shipyards and factories. One district has been rebaptized *Ta Rossika* (The Russians) of late. I don't know what Elefsina's like when all the smokestacks are belching, but it looks to me as though it's in the process of being reborn, sprouting green shoots like Demeter's grains of wheat after a long and harrowing winter. O

How to get there
Take the main road heading west out of Athens towards Corinth and follow the signs to Elefsina.

Where to eat
There are eateries of all sorts on the waterfront, a few blocks south of the site. *To Limanaki*, a fish taverna, is the best of the lot.

1 *Waterfront, Elefsina*
2 *The museum*
3 *The remaining karyatid*
4 *Ancient and modern Elefsina*

The slow road to Delphi

I'd like to take you on the slow road to Delphi… Sounds like a song, doesn't it? Full of promise and romance. And that it will be, though you will have to use your imagination, just a little bit. This is about detours – pleasant asides that will delay your arrival at the navel of the ancient world – but which may hold a truer, more personal satisfaction, all the more precious because you'll be on your own. No tour buses will be lined up end-to-end like a chain of voracious caterpillars to 'devour' the walls of Aigosthena, the museum of Thebes or the oracle at Livadia.

Getting onto this route involves heading out of Athens on the road to Corinth. At Elefsina you leave the great, green, greasy bay behind and take to the hills, following the signs to Thiva on your right. As you snake up the two-lane road, consider for a moment that until the early 1960s this was the start of the old national road between Athens and Thessaloniki. The pass itself was exploited from time immemorial by invaders who had rolled down the plain of Thessaly virtually unhindered to pounce on Attica.

As you make your way through pine woods that have mostly escaped the annual summer conflagrations that threaten all greenery in the vicinity of Athens, keep an eye out for signs to Porto Yermeno, our first stop. Here you bypass Vilia, favored before the war as a summer resort because of its healthy climate, and slalom down some 23 km of generous curves to the gulf of Corinth and the castle on its shore.

The castle soon appears above the pines. Its walls stretch across the valley, its two towers loom as high as 12 meters above the walls. Aigosthena is said to be the best preserved ancient fortress in Greece. It was built in the 4th century BC by the Megarans who were allied with Sparta, and they evidently installed a large garrison here to guard this corner of the gulf. But the name is not connected with any battle, nor does an historical event or intriguing legend endow the stones with a story. So you have to make one up. What comes to my mind are the poor soldiers, bored out of their wits at this outpost, pacing the ramparts, scanning the horizons for treacherous triremes, sharpening their spears, inventing bawdy jokes and tall tales to pass the time. Did they play games on the beach? If not beach volley then football with a pinecone? Who sent them packing? Epaminondas and his Thebans, who finally trounced the Spartans? Or Philip's Macedonians? The guidebooks don't tell us. All we know is that later generations pilfered some of its wonderful stones to erect a monastery and that even those buildings have crumbled, leaving only a small chapel amongst the ruined fortifications.

You can trace the walls into the sea, have a swim and a snack at the summer colony of Porto Yermeno, which pays absolutely no heed to the monument at its side, and then drive back up to the main road.

A bit further on, nearer the top of the hill, another set of walls juts importantly from amidst the scrub and pines. They belong to the 4th century BC fort of Eleutherai; you can see how strategic the Kaza pass was considered then. Many centuries later, the Nazis and the Communists also found it useful. The snow poles at the sides of the road warn us that, close as it is to Athens, this road is often blocked in winter.

A more poignant set of stones awakens other memories. With not even a sign to identify the spot, a few tumbled, scattered blocks of masonry are all that remains of Plataia, a city-state whose men are remembered for their gallant fight against the Persians at Marathon and Thermopylai. If Herodotus hadn't written about them, we would never have known. The far-flung stones in a half-mown field at the foot of

Mt. Kithairon only tell us about the impermanence of what we build to last forever – Shelley's Ozymandias syndrome.

Here we've crossed into Boeotia (Viotia, nowadays), a land of gently swelling hills patterned like an afghan blanket in squares of yellow, green, and brown. A solitary tree on the ridge sets a scale to measure them by. In the 19th century, English Philhellenes, such as Cardinal Newman, had little praise for this landscape, calling it dull and "notorious for the very want of the special purity, elasticity, clearness and salubrity of the air of Attica." Even its fertility came under censure, with Arnold Toynbee remarking that "by providing an insufficient challenge, it ensured that the inhabitants could never achieve a cultural response of Athenian magnitude." Nevertheless, for all its dullness, Thebes and the area around it may perhaps be the oldest continuously inhabited spot in all Europe.

Anyone brought up on legends of the Sphinx and Oedipus, however, is bound to be disappointed by a

3

visit to Thebes, modern day Thiva. There are no spooky ruins where we can speculate on what went on in Jocasta's bedroom, no high walls where Antigone's ghost still raves. The modern town is apparently squatting on top of the Mycenaean, Classical and even Byzantine Thebes. And just one tower exists from the days when Thebes was the capital of the Duchy of Athens and knights astride caparisoned steeds jousted for milady's favor on the plain below. The idea of 13th-century Thebans weaving exquisite silks and talking of courtly love boggles the mind, but it was among the most treasured possessions of Frankish Greece.

The tower is still the town's most distinctive landmark. Luckily for us, the museum is right under it and therefore easy to locate. But before you go inside, pay attention to the marble fragments in the courtyard. Though unlabelled, many are reliefs from Frankish and earlier churches; some depict peacocks and winged horses, while a delightful mosaic shows less exalted creatures – ducks, roosters and owls – in bright simplicity.

The slow
road to
Delphi

The exhibits inside are even more interesting, for the museum at Thiva has one of the best provincial collections in this country. There are a couple of sweet-smiling archaic *kouroi*, touching gravestones showing bereaved families and mournful hounds, beautiful little statuettes from Hercules' funeral pyre on Mt. Iti, Mycenaean lapis lazuli jewelry, graceful Tanagra figurines, a satyr grinning gleefully at his glorious erection and, most impressive of all, a room full of unique clay sarcophagi, painted between 1400 and 1200 BC. This museum is not to be missed, and visiting is easy. The museum is open longer than most, from 8:30 am to 7 pm on weekdays, closing at 3 pm on Saturdays and Sundays.

At Livadia, our next stop, follow the signs for the '*pighés*' as you drive through town (left instead of right for Delphi). Here, on the banks of the ancient springs of Lethe and Mnemosyne, Forgetting and Memory, you can give your imagination a rest, if you choose, and simply enjoy a refreshing drink under the plane trees overlooking a pond spanned by a

> We've crossed into Boeotia, a land of gently swelling hills patterned like an afghan blanket in squares of yellow, green and brown.

old stone bridge dating from Ottoman times. Livadia is busy remodeling its rivers into miniscule cascades and millponds lined with shaded cafés. It's a setting so pretty and so watery you cannot believe it's part of the same dusty market town you have just driven through.

Sipping something cool, you can put your fancy into high gear and try to picture what the district round the springs must have been like when the Oracle of Trophonios was in business. Trophonios was a son of a king of Orchomenos and, with his brother Agamedes, was said to have been the architect of the very first temple to Apollo at Delphi. The two also liked to help themselves to the contents of a treasury they'd built, until one day, when Agamedes was caught. Fearful that he'd spill the beans, Trophonios sliced off his brother's head. Immediately, the earth split open and swallowed him up. You'd have thought that would be the end of him but somehow he burrowed as close to the surface as he could get and there began to utter prescient moans about the future. In time, this oracle became second in fame and popularity only to that of Pythia at Delphi, despite the ordeal associated with eliciting advice.

For if a man wanted to understand these arcane mumblings he had to subject himself to the same fate, so Pausanias, the intrepid guidebook writer of the 2nd century AD, tells us. Thus, after many purification rituals, baths and examining of entrails, he had to insert himself feet first into a kiln-shaped pit. Once his knees were through, a tremendous force would suck him down through a deep channel and then spit him out again "through the sacred mouth." Then, the priests sat him, "still possessed with terror" and barely conscious, on the Throne of Memory where he recounted what he had learned. "Later," Pausanias writes, "he comes to his senses no worse than before, and can laugh again… I am not writing from hearsay, as I have consulted Trophonios and have seen others do so."

Today, no such terror lingers in the canyon and cliffs that form a dramatic backdrop to Livadia, and I was too hot to climb in search of the oracle. Instead I sat under the plane trees and contemplated the ruins of yet another fortress from below. This one, in pretty good condition, was erected by the Catalan Grand Company, a band of ruffians and mercenaries who took over Boeotia from the Frankish nobles in 1311 and held on for another sixty years.

Thinking about all the extraordinary armies, legendary figures and adventurers that have left their imprint on Boeotia, it seems anything but dull. And if these places eventually succumb to a tourist invasion, let's just be grateful it's been a slow road that got them there.

1 *Livadia*
2,4 *Aigosthena*
3 *Plataia*

Orchomenos and Livadia:
old stones, new life

The first time I headed north looking for Lake Kopais, I missed it completely because of course there was no water. This interminable flat Boeotian plain was drained by a Scottish engineering firm between the late 1880s and 1931 and was in fact owned by the British until the Greek government expropriated it after the Civil War. Others had tried to reclaim the rich black soil – Alexander and Hadrian, for example – but only once before had Greece's largest lake been dry, more than three thousand years ago in Mycenaean times. A tribe called the Minyans, about whom not much is known, devised a system of dikes and canals that diverted the water to various sink holes (*katavothres*) that sucked it underground and eventually out to sea. It was a feat worthy of Hercules and just one indication of how clever and powerful the Minyans were.

Orchomenos' pride and joy is the treasury of Minyas, the largest tomb yet discovered in Greece.

P ausanias, that doctor from Asia Minor who crisscrossed the Greek mainland in the 2nd century AD, meticulously noting all the monuments, legends and gossip, tells us that their capital, Orchomenos, was "as famous and glorious as any city in Greece." And that its ruler, Minyas, "had such an income that he was wealthier than all his predecessors and was the first man known to us who built a treasure house to keep his riches in."

There is no hint of riches in Orchomenos today. Lying at the northwest end of the Kopais plain, it's a drab collection of flat-topped concrete houses, which on this blustery winter day are not even redeemed by the usual flowering vines and carnations in old oil tins. The road to it runs straight as an arrow between furrowed fields of black earth, waiting for the next crops of thirsty cotton and corn to be sown. Along the verge, straggly stalks tufted with shreds of dingy fluff that didn't make it to the gins give the empty landscape an even more bedraggled air. The flush of prosperity that has transformed agricultural outposts like Trikala, Karpenissi, Lamia and Larissa seems to have bypassed Orchomenos. But do not despair, there's more to it than meets the eye.

If you had come with Pausanias, you would have seen a 4th century BC theater, carved out of the hillside, with a succession of temples rising above it up to the walls and gates of the town the Macedonians built and the acropolis with a venerable fort. Of the temples, only the foundations can be seen, but the theater has twelve to thirteen rows of seats in a reasonable state of preservation. The fortress is in good condition, too, they say and worth the climb, especially on a clear day.

The town's pride and joy, however, is the Treasury of Minyas, a beehive tomb larger even than Agamemnon's at Mycenae, which means it is the largest yet discovered in Greece. It was still intact in the 2nd century, when Pausanias called it "one of the greatest wonders of Greece and of the world… They say that the topmost stone is a keystone holding the entire building in place." Originally it was covered in earth like the tombs at Vergina, but many of its awesome hewn blocks were appropriated by later building contractors and only the entrance, topped by a Stonehengian slab of grey marble, still stands to its full height. Inside the tomb there is a *thalamos* or inner chamber, hollowed from solid rock, the carved

ceiling of which reflects Minyan talent for smaller works of art, decorated as it is with a double perimeter of rosettes enclosing swirling spirals and fan-shaped leaves. The notion that the rosettes may symbolize poppies adds a hint of possible hedonism to the austere ruin. The only other ornament is a large statue base, about a meter wide and 4 meters long. Of much later date, it may have held statues of Philip II, Alexander the Great and other family members. Found nearby was a stone incised with the names of cavalrymen from Orchomenos who followed Alexander to Persia and actually managed to return. The list cannot be very long.

The palace of Minyas is said to have stood across the street, within the precincts of the splendid Byzantine church of the Dormition of the Virgin (*Koimisi tis Theotokou*) or *Panayia*. This is the other reason for paying a visit to Orchomenos. Erected in 874, it is not only the oldest church in Boeotia (Viotia) but also the only one of its kind in Greece. The design follows a Bulgarian prototype, but to me its facade is even more interesting than its shape. Its front consists of a double layer of perfectly round column drums, recycled from a temple to the Graces that was the site's first structure. Numerous square and rectangular ancient blocks form the lower courses, while the sides and rear are studded with Early Christian and ancient carvings, from animal and floral patterns to inscriptions, and even a sundial set off by delicate peacocks. In fact there is so much writing incorporated in the masonry that the church used to be called Skripou from the Latin *scriptus*.

Sadly, the interior of the church is encumbered by scaffolding, its graceful arched windows blocked with styrofoam panels. The priest who unlocked the door to give us a quick look at the blackened frescoes and icon screen told us that the damage was not the work of long-ago Turks but of "Satanists" on Christmas Day, 1995. "They broke the windows, stole relics and then set fire to the church. They were never caught." To be honest, some of the cement neo-Orthodox horrors with egg-shaped domes that lie half-finished in traditional settings arouse vandalistic impulses even in this law-abiding citizen, but to harm a splendid old monument like this one is a real crime against Greece's heritage.

Livadia

There being nothing more to keep us in Orchomenos, not even a worthy taverna, we set off for Livadia, its traditional rival in ancient times, a short drive away. Not so long ago, in the early 70s when I first passed through Livadia on the way to Delphi, it was simply a busy market town with tractors clogging the narrow streets, hunkered beneath precipitous cliffs and blessed by swiftly rushing streams. The waters gave it a certain charm, not least because of their names, for these are the ancient springs of Lethe and Mnemosyne (Forgetting and Memory). Now you could call it the jewel of Viotia. It has reinvented itself, transforming old watermills that used to grind wheat into beautiful restaurants and cafés, landscaping the riverbanks into plane-tree-shaded oases, and even scaping the water into ponds and cataracts. What's more, this initiative seems to be largely the work of an imaginative, efficient municipality and the Helikon Development Society, SA, using funds from the Leader II program. Bravo! It is not often we see EU money being so well spent.

The latest addition to Livadia's renaissance is its Historical and Ethnological Museum, which opened in 2000. Set underneath the sloping square, it is so discreet as to be virtually invisible; the only clue to its existence a sign pointing down some steps next to a large waterwheel. Although it was well past noon on

Old stones, new life

Livadia has reinvented itself, transforming old watermills into beautiful restaurants and cafés and landscaping the riverbanks into shaded oases.

Sunday, the staff were preparing for a new exhibition of local costumes in this converted factory. Surrounding them lovingly laid-out showcases of agricultural and industrial equipment illustrated Livadia's past role as an important textile manufacturing center.

Opposite, water pours from one side of the Neromylo. Now a restaurant, this was a working *dristella* not long ago, where *flokatis* were washed and fluffed. Further upstream, beyond the cafés, beyond a medieval tower with Classical masonry, are votive niches in the rock and a chamber with benches, maybe an ancient bath house of sorts for ritual ablutions in the springs. But on summer evenings, the biggest attraction here is the amphitheater built into an opening in the gorge, which hosts performances from ancient drama to rock concerts, classical music and ballet.

On a less exalted level, Livadia has attained distinction locally as a mecca for carnivores. Vegetarians may have to subsist on fried potatoes and Greek salads, but meat-eaters will be in seventh heaven. A friend's grandfather and his brother-in-law once devoured 7 kilos of roast kid in one sitting and they weren't even competing. At Easter, when the whole country goes on a meat-eating binge, Livadia's main square is one big barbecue pit. You might want to make a note that, in the legendary Greek tradition of hospitality to strangers, the town makes a point of having enough lambs spinning on spits to feed any visitors for free.

Ravenous after a morning of ruminating over Minyan mysteries, we didn't quite match those old Livadians, but certainly tucked away more than our share of delectable chops. It's wonderful when a place can modernize gracefully while still holding onto the best of the past. **O**

How to get there

Take the National Road north as far as Kastro, where there are signs for Orchomenos, and bear left once in the town – where there are no signs – and ask someone to point you in the direction of the antiquities (*Ta archaia*) and the Church of the Panayia. The road to Livadia (6 km) is the one that passes between the church and the ancient theater. The drive from Athens to Orchomenos (125 km) should not take more than 1 1/2 hours.

Where to have lunch

At the lower end of Livadia's lovely elongated square, the converted *Neromylos* came highly recommended, but since it had been commandeered by a conclave of local politicos, we had to be (and were) content with the less stylish grill house, known to all as *Ta Souvlakia*, next door. Here we feasted on excellent lamb and pork chops, souvlakia, *kokoretsi*, salads and fried potatoes accompanied by a wine that went down very well, all served by a congenial waiter who didn't seem to mind running in and out with refills. Among the cafés, *Xenia* is the oldest and most attractive.

1 *Church of the Panayia*
2,4 *Livadia*
3 *Church of the Panayia, detail*

The mountains of Nafpaktia

In the old days, even fifteen years ago, you had to be tough to venture into most of Greece's mountains. And I don't mean just to walk or hike amongst the glorious peaks or verdant upper pastures. Surviving the nights in a bleak unheated room under a pile of scratchy blankets required even sterner stuff. The tavernas were invariably enclosed by plate-glass windows more suitable for balmy climates, the penetrating chill dulled by a small potbellied stove and immoderate quantities of rough local wine. Often we slept fully clothed. I have fond memories of those times, though I'm not sure I want to repeat them.

There are signs that a revolution is taking place in formerly remote mountain regions.

These days one doesn't have to suffer. There are signs that a revolution is taking place in formerly remote mountain regions. The population may have moved out, but in the past decade weekenders are moving in, attracted by comfortable, cozy hotels, eateries with fireplaces and café-bars where espresso is more popular than a *vari glyko*.

In the Vardoussia range above Nafpaktos – a wild area of precipitous peaks, dense fir forests and a smattering of deserted villages – this revolution is especially evident and all the more surprising for being so unexpected. Oreini Nafpaktia has always been one of Greece's poorest regions, along with Epirus. It was also as untamed as the Agrafa, whose very name means 'unwritten' and is synonymous with being untaxable, as the Turks found these districts to be. But even if taxes had been collectible, what would have been the tariff on the potatoes, timber, honey and *tsipouro* that were Nafpaktia's main products? In fact, people were its chief exports. Some men travelled around Greece, selling their skills as masons; others worked in factories, while many, many villagers wound up in the United States.

Funnily enough, the revival in Ano Hora is the last chapter in a typical Greek-strikes-it-rich-in-America story. Fifty years ago, with five dollars in his pocket, Yiorgos Papaioannidis sailed off to Ellis Island, spent a few years working on the railroads and then took himself off to Cleveland, where he eventually opened a restaurant. He named it the Crystal. Before long he owned five or six restaurants and had made enough money to return to his native land. He opened a hotel in Athens and called it Crystal, too, and then decided to do the same in Ano Hora. The village elders designated a site at the entrance to Ano Hora, and building started. That was ten years ago. Yiorgos lived to see its first 20 rooms inaugurated and baptized it. You could call this third Crystal, expanded to sixty rooms in what some would call the middle of nowhere, *to xenodoheio tou trellou* or the madman's hotel, but his dream was to bring life back to his languishing hamlet. And with his grandsons, Thanasis and Andreas, in charge and introducing modern concepts, the dream doesn't seem such a folly.

Crystal is full almost every weekend. In autumn, many of its patrons are hunters, who come with their dogs to track down wild boar fattened on the district's chestnuts. Mushrooms, wild strawberries and alpine flowers could be other incentives for making the trip if basking in the shade of inaccessible mountains were not sufficient. Whatever the reason, the number of adventurers is growing so fast that two more hotels have opened in Ano Hora, and there is a small hotel in each of the neighboring villages of Terpsithea, Ambelakiotissa and Kato Hora. Meanwhile, Ano Hora also has a sprin-

"Being below can be better than being above," one man from the lower village said.

kling of new tavernas and bars, where the fare is not only splendid but varied. Yes, there is the usual bean soup and grilled lambchops, but you can also find superb cheese and greens pies – one *hortopita* was the best I've ever bitten into – delectable *lachano* (cabbage) *dolmades*, chicken soup so thick it resembles risotto, and of course wild boar *stifado*, chops and ribs, supplied by a farm, not caught in the woods.

It must be said that these villages cannot be compared to Epirus's Zagorohoria, whose stalwart stone houses are architectural jewels. Here the slate roofs have almost all been replaced by red tiles, and almost all of them have wooden balconies, painted in colors more common to Mykonos, from powderpuff blue and emerald green to pompadour pink. Although many of them are in reasonably good condition, the emptiness that surrounds them can bring on a fit of melancholy. Not so long ago Ano Hora had 5,000 permanent inhabitants, now there are sixteen, not counting the hotel staff. Kato Hora, once bustling with the gossip of 400 people, now has only two, the forest ranger and his wife. Our first impression was one of abandonment and filled us with dismay. We thought of strangling the friends whose enthusiasm had brought us so far. But by the time we'd had lunch and talked to a few amiable locals in Ano Hora, they were in our good graces again.

After breakfast, clutching the detailed map of walks and drives provided by the hotel, we set off on one of the pilgrimages practically every visitor to the area makes. Ambelakiotissa, about 15 kilometers away, is home to a monastery with a famous icon. Apparently, during the Ottoman conquest of Thessaly in the 15th century, the fighting was so intense that the icon, which had been happily hanging in a church in Ambelakia, spirited itself out of danger and wound up in the woods above the village, then and until fairly recently called Kozitsa. There it radiated an otherworldly glow which eventually caught the notice of a passerby. The icon is reputedly the creation of St. Luke and, like the other paintings attributed to him, it is almost entirely covered with intricately worked gold sheeting, which could easily have shone like a beacon, given a little sunlight. Whether you believe in miracles or not, it is quite beautiful, and occupies pride of place next to the monastery's other treasure, the forearm of St. Polycarp of Smyrna, also swathed in gold. The most remarkable thing about this tale, however, was that it was told to me by a woman who appears to commute between Kozitsa and Sydney.

After delivering a short sermon on the superiority of Orthodoxy to other religions, she darted down the hill to the village proper, not even bothering to follow the path. We caught up with her again as she was leaving the café/general store. There three old men sat silently in a room too big and empty to be welcoming. They perked up at the sight of new faces and told us the village would be packed as soon as the temperatures rose and families started coming up from Nafpaktos. They said that fifteen people lived here year round, but besides an old woman clucking to her unresponsive goat we didn't see another soul.

Because of the monastery, though, the road to Kozitsa is, surprisingly, fully asphalted. I say surprisingly because it's rare to find more than a dirt track in such isolated places. It weaves and slithers through thick fir forests and groves of plane trees, providing glimpses of sharp, snow-streaked summits and distant hamlets. But sometimes it seems to teeter on the brink of the Kakavos gorge that slices through the crags separating Kozitsa and Ano Hora.

"Too close for comfort," muttered Andreas Angelopoulos, owner of Xenios, the only hotel in Kato Hora. "I've done that trip once, and that's enough for me, brings on my vertigo."

Xenios, an attractive handful of log cabins clustered around a stone building decorated with tasteful rusticity, looks like wilderness retreats I've seen in the Adirondacks or Yellowstone Park. But Andreas took his inspiration from Finland, where he worked for several years. His vision for Kato Hora was originally his father-in-law's, another returnee from the United States with an ache in his heart for his ancestral home.

The mountains
of Nafpaktia

"He died before we fixed up the house, which was built in the 18th century, but he passed on his love of the place to me. Psychologically," Andreas went on, "it takes you a moment to adjust to the idea that being below can be better than being above, but our view of Ano Hora is far better than their view of us." We followed his gaze up the mountain and had to agree.

Over a thimble of *tsipouro*, we took up another subject with Andreas, too delicate to discuss with a real local but intriguing nonetheless. This district, Kravara by name, became famous or infamous thanks to a novel by Andreas Karkavitsas in the early 20th century. Called *O Zitianos* (The Beggar), it described a caste of professional beggars, who used to invade the cities during holidays, and indeed traveled all over Greece to ply their trade. Patrick Leigh Fermor devotes a whole chapter to them in *Roumeli* and even learned their language, invented to outwit both police and targets. "The true Kravarite vocation was straight mendiancy; but mendiancy elaborated by many ruses: feigned blindness, madness and epileptic fits, and, above all, the semblance of lameness, loss of limb and malformation. Some would be hunch-backs… Others contorted their arms… some even pretended to have lost both legs, or, at least, the use of them." He goes on to say that some villages were "mountain academies of begging" for "these disguises achieved a perfection which was not learnt overnight."

When asked, any native of Kravara will quickly change the subject and no doubt the caste has gone the way of the dodo. But such a creative approach to the pressures of poverty, combined with the humor revealed by Leigh-Fermor, left me more inclined to admire than condemn.

As we left, Andreas pointed us to another scenic road, paved most of the way, to Kryoneri. He was the second person to tell us that this road, which peters out, hiccups over rutted tracks and crosses river beds as it passes through dazzling scenery, is a favorite with Israeli tourists. They arrive in convoys of rented jeeps and bounce and careen all the way north to Karditsa. I can sympathize with their thirst for untamed wilderness and adventure without bullets and suicide bombers, but how did they find out about it? If word of Kravara's beauty has spread as far as Israel, we Athenians had better get a move on. ⚙

How to get there

The quickest route from Athens to Oreini Nafpaktia/Kravara is via the national road to Patras and the Rio-Antirrio ferry to Nafpaktos. From there turn east as far as Kato Dafni, where the road winds north to Limnitsa, Terpsithea, Elatou and Ano Hora. We took the longest way, heading for Lidoriki and the Mornos Dam from Galaxidi, below Delphi on the Gulf of Corinth, and from there to the mountain villages. We returned via Nafpaktos and the road that runs along the coast as far as Itea. Ano Hora is about 75 minutes from Nafpaktos. The whole trip takes a minimum of four hours, one way.

Where to stay

Crystal Guesthouse, Ano Hora, tel. 26340 41555-7, fax 26340 41558. A double room with breakfast will cost less during the week than on weekends.

Xenios, Kato Hora, tel. 26340 41111, fax 26340 41112, email: xenioskh@otenet.gr, website: www.xenios-katohora.gr. You can take a double room in the main building or join up with friends and rent a cabin for two couples with livingroom and fireplace.

Where to eat

Both *Crystal* and *Xenios* have excellent restaurants serving local specialties. In Ano Hora the restaurant with no name but known as *Vassili's place* in the middle of the main street (opposite the antique bus) has splendid food at very reasonable prices and posters of Switzerland on the walls, which could be the Vardoussia mountains. At the end of the street, also on the left but entered from the terrace above it, *To Platano* looked like a good place to eat. Both have fireplaces.

1-2 *Ano Hora*
3-4 *Ambelakiotissa*
5 *The Vardoussia mountains*

Pelion's appleland

Updating a guide book is frustrating and exhausting business; exhausting because you have to check old claims and unearth new 'discoveries' in the shortest possible time, and frustrating because stunning landscapes and intriguing curiosities flash by your bug-spattered windshield and you can't spare a moment to get out and savor them.

In any other country, there'd be banners saying "welcome to Appleland," juice stalls, bumper stickers and Granny Smith balloons.

'Doing' Pelion last week, therefore, was a torture. I hadn't been to the centaurs' mountain in seven years and instead of looking for the perfect doorstop among the smooth white stones at Mylopotamos; paddling in the azure waves at Horefto; or pursuing the Theofilos trail in the cafés and churches of Makrinitsa – I had to inspect hotel rooms, chase up bus schedules and cross off defunct restaurants. Nonetheless, my chauffeur and I did enjoy ourselves. Pelion in spring (summer, fall, winter) is so beautiful and full of eye-catching vistas and ear-thrilling bird- and brook-song that even driving briskly through it was a pleasure.

But you can read about Pelion's more obvious attractions in any tourist brochure. Let me tell you what else I discovered on my whirlwind visit.

First, let it be known that we whirled at something less than dervish speed, for no one can circulate really quickly on the mountain. Most of the roads are still narrow and snaky, so we spent a tense quarter of an hour chugging uphill from Volos in the wake of two asthmatic tour buses. This gave us plenty of opportunity to watch the view unfold over the city and the Pagasitic Gulf and to note with surprise that the greenery is rampant even before one reaches the city limits.

2

Anakassia, the first village, is home to a museum of paintings by Theofilos. That itinerant artist from Lesvos traipsed around Pelion for thirty years, costumed variously in a *fustanella* or as Alexander the Great, paying for his food and shelter by painting scenes from Greek history on café walls. Alas, it had closed for the day, so we rejoined the procession towards Portaria and Makrinitsa – Pelion's most visited, being most accessible, villages.

My guidebook says that they've succumbed to commercialism. But the few *fastfoodadika* and pseudo-traditional buildings were not nearly as upsetting as the clamor created by a full-scale invasion of fourteen-year-olds on a class outing. Smoking on side streets, shrieking louder than their blaring ghetto blasters, they made it just a tad difficult to concentrate on the Pelion formula for atmosphere: three-story mansions, venerable plane-tree-shaded squares, gurgling fountains and slate-roofed churches, not to mention Makrynitsa's excellent folklore musuem. Overwhelmed by tourists and teenagers, the villagers have responded by giving them what they think they want. But if kitsch and commercialism irk you, Pelion still lags far behind Bavaria, and the back lanes crisscrossing the steep slopes over which the villages spread in all directions are still quiet, impenetrable to cars, and unspoiled.

Zagora, Pelion's biggest village, is another story altogether. Because it's the apple-growing capital of Greece, the state has designated it an agricultural district and given the locals no help in attracting tourists. This means that the National Tourist Organization has ignored it, but this official neglect makes it all the more appealing. Zagora is a real village, with tractors and pickups parked higgledly-piggledy on the busy main thoroughfare wherever it suits their owners. It is home to grocery and hardware stores instead of shops selling key chains and post cards. In any other country, there'd be banners saying "welcome to Appleland," juice stalls, bumper stickers and Granny Smith balloons. We were grateful for their absence.

But there is no reason why Zagora should not be on every tourist itinerary. It's got four of the requisite Pelion churches *cum* spacious shaded *plateias*. The one around Agios Georgios is among Pelion's most impressive, offering wonderful views of Horefto on the white beach below and interesting non-ecclesiastical architecture, including some beautifully restored 18th century mansions and several 19th century industrial buildings that need rescuing.

It's hard to conceive that two centuries ago Zagora was a prosperous silk-producing community whose ships, anchored at Horefto, carried the

155

valuable fabric to Egypt, Smyrna, and Northern Europe. Now 16-wheelers from Holland and Germany lurch round its hairpin turns laden with some of its 20,000 tons of apples. The red, blue, and yellow crates used to pack them lie in splendid disarray around the refrigerator plants halfway down the mountain; from above they look like giant flower beds.

The Gayiannis *Archontiko* (mansion) just below St. George's Square is a vestige of Zagora's silk days. Built in 1780, it resembles the stately homes in Makrinitsa, Vyzitsa and other Pelion villages, which still have a fortified look about them. In fact, when refugees fled from Constantinople to Pelion after 1453, the rich among them constructed their houses like fortresses for protection against the Turks. As trade brought wealth and privileges, the mansions became proclamations of a very comfortable life style Nikos Gayiannis, a former tunnel engineer who worked all over the world before returning to Zagora, opened it as a hotel in 1993. As we followed him into the stone-walled ground floor where once the wine, olive oil and charcoal were stored and up the solid but creaky stairs, he put a finger to his lips. "Ssshhhh, some guests are sleeping," he whispered, pointing to the heavy carved doors. The second floor with its low sculpted ceilings and tiled fire-

places was the family's winter quarters; in summer they moved to the airy third floor which has stained-glass fanlights above the windows that send rainbow bands onto the white walls. Back down in the kitchen, a separate building where guests are served breakfast, Nikos told such tales of Christmas parties without electricity but with the old double oven gloriously roaring that I wanted to come back in winter.

A half hour in Sotos's photo shop on the main street revealed other facets of this storied region. A self-taught photographer who abandoned Athens for Zagora, Sotos makes postcards of his favorite shots in all weathers. Many

were of magical places I know I'll never see, like Ai Lia, an old church near a rushing brook above Agia Paraskevi, the first of the village's four squares, so high above the main road the locals call it Perahora (beyond town). I pored over the grimy faces of charcoal makers, a battered beach during and after a squall, the silence of a snow-muffled trail, a lethal looking red mushroom, ferns in the mist....

When I talked to Ingrid Brink I felt like calling a halt to any further travel, ever. Sitting in the courtyard of Villa Horizonte, which doubles as a mini-amphitheater, she told me about the summer programs she and her husband/partner Wolf Keil put together. She's Swedish, he's German, and they moved here from Naxos to set up a cultural center for northeast Pelion. Besides art exhibitions and concerts, they run seminars, music school sessions and conferences well into the autumn. Wolf guides walks and treks at any time of year. As Ingrid said, "We try to collect well known and unknown people, bring them together here, and make things happen that both the locals and outsiders will enjoy."

Fittingly, Villa Horizonte – whose horizons on a clear day include Mount Athos to the north and the scattered Sporades – is located close to the so-called Rigas Ferreos Secret School, where Orthodox priests kept culture alive during the Turkish occupation. We used it as a base for the guide book research. For the next day and a half we dipped like butterflies into pretty coves and beaches south and west of Zagora, passing judgment, taking notes and flitting on to the next destination.

While the level of development at Horefto is still acceptable, at Agios Ioannis it is unredeemably tacky, though the beaches at either end of it are umbrella-free. Mylopotamos, Pelion's most photographed twin bays, is untouched and its two tavernas are excellent, but the picturesque portlet of Damouhari has become a construction site for villas, bungalows and hotels. Nevertheless, the twenty or so Germans dancing the *kalamatiano* at the beach taverna were enjoying their Greek experience. In the afternoon, they planned to climb up the *kalderimi* (cobbled path) to Tsangarada, a village so concealed by greenery it seems only to exist in tiny clusters. I felt more content in Kissos, just above it, where I could take in everything at a glance. The cozy, friendly Ksenonas Kissos was just as welcoming as it was when I had a memorable birthday party there in 1990.

On we pushed as if pursued by harpies. Through the empty stretch after Tsangarada, where hills rolled with golden stubble and prickly scrub, and sweet-scented broom replaced the ferns and fruit trees. It seemed an age before we reached Argalasti, the no-frills center of southern Pelion. Here too there were few concessions to

Pelion's
appleland

tourism, except for the Centavros Farm Riding Treks posters pasted on every telephone pole. As I chatted with the owner's mother over a lemonade in Sokaki taverna, whose walls are a collage of riders and ponies on fabulous trails, I daydreamed for an instant about exploring Pelion on horseback.

Argalasti is on the saddle between the Aegean and Pagasitic coasts. On the Aegean side is Paltsi where we know there are divine beaches beloved of German campers, on the Gulf side is Melina where we once spent an idyllic week camping illicitly in an olive grove. From Melina a new road runs all the way to Trikeri, all by itself at the end of the peninsula. The Pagasitic shore of Pelion is pretty but domesticated. Calm and unruffled by the rocks and waves that make the Aegean coast so dramatic and invigorating, it seems more conventionally Greek, with olive trees far outnumbering apples and chest-

Once at the Villa Horizonte I felt like calling a halt to any further travel, ever.

nuts. Little blue tables line the seafront, ready to welcome evening diners, but not a cove remains without a house, hotel or restaurant.

We sped along the new road, finished in 1997, reaching the village in about 20 minutes. Because Trikeri was so remote – for centuries its only communication with the rest of the world was by boat – it always held a fascination for me. Now there's no mystery, just a sleepy unpretentious village without a real beach. The locals talked excitedly about a big hotel going up and changing their lives.

The last day we checked on the restored mansions at Vyzitsa, the wonderful bakery at Milies and the famous *trenaki*, finally put back into service on weekends to the delight of children of all ages. The restored turn-of-the-(20th) century choochoo and three wooden coaches make the 16 km run from Ano Lehonia on the coast through superb scenery to Milies for a very modest fee, round trip. Not every concession to tourism is an abomination. **O**

How to get there

Mount Pelion can be visited by bus or private car from Volos, about 4 1/2 hours drive north of Athens.

Where to stay

The places mentioned in the article have the following phone numbers: The *Gayiannis Archontiko Hotel*, 24260 23391; *Villa Horizonte*, 24260 23342; *Ksenonas Kissos*, 24260 31214; *Kentavros Farm*, 24230 54439, 54131. *Villa Drakopoulou*, also on St. George's Square in Zagora, 24260 23566, opened after this article was published. Another *archontiko* turned into an attractive hotel, it is run by the village Women's Cooperative.

Where to eat

In Horefto, *Gorgones* has been serving fine food since 1878(!), while *Delfinia*, open winter and summer, specializes in *mezedes* to help the *tsipouro* go down, plus lots of fresh fish. In Zagora, *Meidani*, run by Kyria Niki, is a good place to taste Pelion *mezedes* while drinking in the view from a flower-filled balcony. In Kissos, do not miss *Makis*, the best restaurant in eastern Pelion. Makis's mother, Kyria Stathoula, uses only the freshest ingredients and rolls out *fyllo* for her fantastic *pites* right before your eyes.

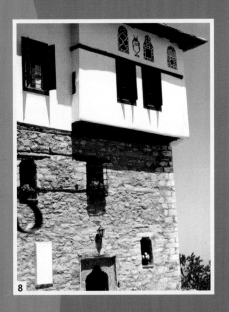

8

1-2 *Damouhari*

3 *Mylopotamos*

4 *View of Agios Ioannis*

5 *View from Villa Horizonte*

6 *Damouhari*

7 *Agios Georgios, Zagora*

8 *The Gayiannis Archontiko*

30

Day
Trips

Nearby Islands

&
Weekends

In search of the real Spetses

Around a hundred years ago, when swimming costumes revealed no mor
than an inch of ankle, some residents of Spetses were so scandalized by th
spectacle of Athenians bathing at one of their beaches that they sowed th
sands with sea urchins to discourage them from ever doing it agair
Nowadays they turn a blasé eye to topless tourists on the town beach, hav
ing long ago learned from whence cometh their livelihood.

Forty years ago, when I arrived in Spetses, the pace was deliciously lazy and romantic. It was set by horse and buggy.

Forty years ago when I first went to Spetses, it seemed like paradise. It took five hours to get there – hydrofoils had yet to beetle the sea – there were no cars, and the pace, deliciously lazy and romantic, was set by horse and buggy. If you lingered long enough in any of the cafés behind the cannons that give the main port its name (Dappia means 'fortified place'), you would see everyone you wanted to get in touch with, phones being still rare in those days. A room cost 30 drachmas, a Tam Tam maybe 3

and Coca Cola could only be had on the black market. Handsome Big George hustled passengers aboard his kaiki for a swim at Zogeria, while pot-bellied Nikos steered his smaller boat across to Kosta on the Peloponnesos with his right foot. The town was small but cosmopolitan; it was easy to meet people and find out what went on inside those beautiful houses that rose above the high walls enclosing courtyards paved with pebble mosaics. From inside there burst the scent of achingly fragrant lemon trees and jasmine vines, and peals of laughter at jokes told simultaneously in English, French and Greek. At parties in Spetses I met Nobel-prize-winning biochemists, movie stars (Melina, Vivien, Greta), world class journalists, best-selling American novelists, Bulgarian emigrés, titled English backgammon sharks, Greek intellectuals, two husbands, and lots and lots of very good friends.

Despite this illustrious company, life was simple, consisting of daily swims in pristine waters and gluttonous sea urchin feasts, long lunches and long naps. In the evenings we'd watch the landscape turn lavender before deciding whether to walk clear across town to dance at Blueberry Hill or creep furtively onto the roof of the Karnayio to hear Kostas "the Gypsy" Hadzis sing. Several summers went by like this and then my sister-in-law died, her house was sold, and Spetses lost its charm for me.

Only recently have I begun to return to the island, at first dismayed by the changes but also rediscovering aspects that have remained very much the same. In all fairness, these are best appreciated in the spring, after Easter and before mid July, when Athenian suburbanites, yuppies and nouveaux riches indus-

3

The elegant
mansions along
the waterfront
still exude their
mysterious allure.

trialists flock to one of their favorite summer watering holes. At first, its modernity seems all too aggres-sive. Red and white sea taxis charge between Kosta, Dappia and the Old Harbor, the infernal racket of motorbikes resounds down narrow streets, Mercedes cabs compete with the buggies, and an unfinished, out-of-scale church rises right next to the jewel-like 18th century monastery of Agios Nikolaos in the Old Harbor. The extraordinary growth of the town up into the hills, no longer quite so green since the for-est fires of 1990 and 2000, makes a mockery of the island's ancient name, Pityousa or 'pine-covered'.

But the essential character of Spetses is indestructible and the taxis at least (both kinds) can be con-venient, though I hate to admit it. The Dappia remains a magnet, drawing even Old Harbor old-timers who pretend to deplore it. They catch up on the gossip in Stamboli's café, just before the steps leading to the tables fronting the cannons where the frappé drinkers congregate. In the small port below, the voices of kaiki captains still ring out, coaxing passengers to swim at Zogeria, Kosta, and other beaches around the island or across the way. Big George is a bit grizzled but still handsome; Nikos, retired, watch-es from the seawall. Most of the Dappia cafés still make their own *amygdalota*, the delicate almond-paste pyramids for which Spetses is famous.

The island is still easy to get to know. It's small, only 22 square km in area, and though its one and only town has expanded enormously in the past couple of decades, all its tavernas, shops, bars and discos are within walking distance of each other. This has made Spetses nightlife for the young as exciting as a garden in spring to a butterfly; the flitting from *ouzeri* to 70s music bar to pizzeria to barrel winery goes on till early morning on weekends and in summer, as clumps of friends tramp from Blueberry Hill (revamped since my time) all the way to the Figaro disco in the inner Old Harbor, and back again.

By day the elegant mansions along and above the waterfront continue to exude their mysterious allure. Some of the most magnificent appear even larger than they are because they rest upon enormous cisterns, a real necessity on this island which has to import water from the mainland. Many of them date back to the early 19th century, when Spetsiots were making fortunes in shipbuilding, trade and business. Two houses have been turned into museums: the Hadjiyannis Mexis house, which has memorabilia related to the War of Independence, ships' figureheads, and a few antiquities; and Laskarina Bouboulina's, whose inlaid Florentine ceiling, 'European' furniture, and period paintings give us a glimpse of how the upper classes

In search of the real Spetses

lived two hundred years ago. Bouboulina, of course, is the island's most illustrious claim to fame. A very clever woman and dedicated patriot, she managed to get the Turkish government to finance her shipbuilding ventures and then captained her ships in battle against them off the coast of Nafplion. Being the only female admiral in Greek history did not shield her from male vindictiveness, however, and she was murdered in 1825 by a fellow islander.

Another famous Spetsiot, Sotirios Anargyros, had a rags-to-riches story typical of the end of the 19th century. He left the island for New York, went to work at a big tobacco company, married the boss's daughter, and returned a millionaire. He built the Hotel Posidonion, a posh Riviera-type establishment where wealthy Athenians played cards and drank tea for more than seventy years. He also replanted the hillsides with pines and founded the Anargyrios School, modeled along English lines, where Greeks posted abroad used to send their sons for an education. It was here that John Fowles taught English in the late 1950s and set some of the scenes of his novel *The Magus*.

All this money and maritime power made the town of Spetses, and its neighbor Hydra, nothing like the conventional image of a Cycladic *hora*. It is by no means a collection of tiny, snow-white cubes clinging to a windswept peak out of the sight of marauding pirates. But unlike Hydra and most of the Cyclades, Spetses's hills are low and gentle, predominantly green not barren. Before the fire, the slopes were indeed covered with pine trees, and even now seedlings of various sizes are fast replacing them. I still love to walk up to the ridge; there are lots of paths, wild flowers and wild asparagus, and views so riveting I can hardly tear myself away. From up there you can see almost as far as Monemvasia to the south, while the view north is a tapestry of aquamarine coves and inlets, emerald hills, the topaz hulks of Dokos, Trikeri, Hydra and some smaller rocks, and the ultramarine deep dotted with pearl-like sails.

Sometimes I walk down to the beach at Agii Anargyri, the island's longest. Some wine and a bite at either of its two tavernas are welcome after the hike (which is less than two hours from Dappia) and snorkeling is unparalleled in the pink and purple dappled cave where Spetsiot women and children are said to have hidden from the Turks while their men were battling them on the other side of the island. (Kaikis, sea taxis and a bus make Agii Anargyri easier to get to.)

Back in town, I find other things unchanged and delightful. Where else can you watch kaikis being built? Their bare-ribbed orange skeletons stand like monumental sculptures at the entrance to the Baltiza, deep inside the Old Harbor. The walk round the Baltiza to the lighthouse now includes a visit to Natalia Mela's zoo, a landscaped park where her fanciful goats, bulls and Cretan *kri kri* graze, her mermaid poses at water's edge, and her young hero raises the torch of liberty from the rocky point. In her Spetses studio Nata has been turning ordinary objects like spades, chains, bells, and metal rods into extraordinary sculptures since the 60s. Her outdoor museum was given to Spetses by a French heiress to the Schlumberger millions who wanted Nata's creations to have the setting they deserved.

But for a real taste of the Spetses I used to know, I make a point of going in late June or early July to the drama festival sponsored by the Athens Center in the open-air theater above the Anargyrios School. The troupe may be American but their humor and vitality, the audience they attract, and the air, heavy with the scent of pine and rasping cicadas concoct for me those innocent, joyful days of the 1960s.

Greece's first marine archaeology museum

You'd never think from its facade that the Hadjiyannis Mexis mansion in Spetses could possibly house a modern, state-of-the-art museum. Its massive grey walls, its imposing stone staircases and enormous cobbled courtyard cannot have changed much since its owner and his daring sailors were rousting the Turkish fleet from the Argosaronic Gulf. The floors creak as you prowl through the upper rooms, filled with memorabilia from the War of Independence – Revolutionary flags, costumes, muskets and even a metal box reputedly holding

n search
of the real
Spetses

Bouboulina's, the famous lady admiral's, bones. The exhibits and their showcases are more or less typical of local collections all over Greece – interesting enough but in need of a facelift.

The ground floor is something else again. Though covering only about two and half rooms at the moment, a museum opened in 1999 which marks a first for Greece. It is devoted entirely to marine archaeology – finds rescued from the deep. Because this is a discipline that could not have been born without modern technology, it is only fitting that the objects on display are skillfully lit, backed up by clear, informative maps, drawings and texts, and supplemented by a film outlining the various stages of the excavation of one particular shipwreck, a Bronze-Age vessel from Cyprus that sank off Iria, near Nafplion, with its cargo of olive oil from Crete. Finds from a second wreck, dating from about 2200 BC and found off Dokos, will soon be added. ○

How to get there

The southernmost of the Saronic islands, Spetses is only 2 hours from Piraeus by hydrofoil, 5 hours by ferry. Call the Piraeus Port Authority for schedules, 210 4280001. It is also about 3 hours by car from Athens. Take the National Road to the Corinth Canal and from there take the road towards Epidavros. Follow the signs to Kranidi, Porto Heli and Kosta, where you can pick up a sea taxi, ferry or kaiki for the short trip across the channel.

Where to eat

Patralis, west of Dappia in Kounoupitsa, is the island's oldest and best fish restaurant; *Paradise Beach* at Agia Marina is a pleasant, sophisticated place for a genteel lunch; *Roussos* near Agios Mamas has ready cooked dishes and fish at economical prices all year round; while *Nektarios*, at the entrance to Baltiza, is where the locals go for a relaxed, simple dinner.

Where to stay

In the luxury class, the most attractive hotels are *Ta Nissia* (22980 75000) on the waterfront and *Zoe's Club* (22980 74447-8) near Dappia. Moderately priced *Varlamis* (22980 74983) above the Old Harbor and *Villa Christina* (22980 72218) are also convenient and quiet.

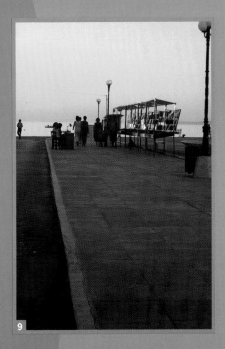

9

1   *The Old Harbor*
2   *Kaiki*
3-4 *Spetses mansions*
5-7 *Typical Spetses features*
  8 *Cave, Agii Anargyri*
  9 *Evening near Dappia*

Southern Evia:
natural park or wind park?

If the Karystos district were on Crete the tour operators would have taken it over long ago. It's got medieval castles and ancient sites, miles of beautiful beaches and leafy mountain villages, living traditions and great tavernas – everything a place needs to become a tourist mecca. Somehow, though, Evia, Greece's second largest island, has been overlooked in the mad rush to develop. Is it too close to the mainland, not island enough? Whatever the reason, we should be grateful such a goldmine lies at our doorstep, just an hour's boat ride from Rafina.

At present there are boats only to Marmari, a burgeoning resort town spreading up the hill behind a wide bay some twenty minutes' drive from Karystos. But if you zigzag up to the main road you become painfully aware that prospectors are already exploiting other natural resources. Southern Evia is rich in stone. Over the past three decades, *petra Karystou* (grey-beige slate) has become the preferred material for terraces, floors and walls in private homes and public areas. The demand was so sudden and so voracious that the road is now a corridor between makeshift depots surrounded by pallets, shards and untidy piles of worked and unworked stone. Evia being even richer in wind, the 'mining' of the air is even more unsightly. Every mountain ridge within sight sports a colonnade of wind generators, massive white totems with arms whirling to turn Boreas into clean electricity. It's true these do not belch thick smoke like the plant at Aliveri in the center of the island, but along with the road grid linking them they cast a pall on this dramatic landscape. And the pylons connecting their power to the substations haven't even been erected yet.

Local opposition is mounting. Demonstrators prevented the last shipload of generators from docking at Marmari or Karystos, so the lorries had to cross over the bridge near Halkis. Installing them will nevertheless continue as government and business are hand in glove. Closer to Karystos graffiti in block letters shout OXI STO NATURA! Saying "No to Nature" sounds like blasphemy and represents attempts by wily entrepreneurs to block the creation of a national park in the large area around Mt. Ohi. This encompasses the mountain range looming behind Karystos and the as yet remote villages and coast bordering the Cavo d'Oro, the channel that separates Evia from Andros. NATURA 2000, the EU program for the protection of natural habitats, would allow for traditional occupations like pasturing of goats and sheep, and even quarrying in some spots, but Aeolian parks and large-scale second home communities have no place in the proposed plan. The case now rests before the Supreme Court of Appeal.

Meanwhile, nature still has the upper hand. Streams gushing from the mountainside swathe the lower slopes of Ohi in green even in late summer. Nightingales, blackbirds, warblers and finches trill from thick tangles of blackberry brambles, stout-branched plane trees and fruit trees of all sorts. Verdant villages like Myli, Aetos, Grabia and Kalyvia bring to mind Andrew Marvell's "The Garden": "annihilating all that's made into a green thought in a green shade." Rare peonies grow in a field near Mekounida, a pair of eagles nest in the Frankish Castello Rosso, a house owl is no rarity. Higher up Ohi and to the east stands a chestnut forest, north of it the wooded Dimosaris gorge runs 10 kilometers down to the sea. Paths link all these places, passing Turkish fountains, old stone bridges, Byzantine churches and a Roman aqueduct along the way.

A strange sight, and one probably unique to Ohi, is less than an hour's walk above Myli. Here, at the remains of a Roman marble quarry, lie several columns up to 12 meters in length, tossed like a titan's pick-up sticks. One or two are unfinished, waiting to be freed from the stone. The site is so steep that when I first saw it, I concluded that the workers forgot to plan ahead and had no way to transport the columns to their destination. But I have since learned that Karystos marble columns stand in Hadrian's Library and the Roman Agora in Athens and were shipped to adorn palaces, villas, temples and forums throughout Italy. Later quarries provided marble for San Marco's in Venice, St. Peter's in Rome, Agia Sophia in Constantinople and – wait for this – the New York Public Library.

At the peak itself looms something even stranger, the so-called Dragon's House or Drakospito. Scholars are unable to agree as to whether it was a place of worship or a sort of beacon tower, and date estimates range from the 13th to the 3rd century BC. It consists of massive rectangular stones that only dragon-slayers could hoist, but what really distinguishes it is a roof of inconceivably large, overlapping slabs arranged on a slant like giant shingles. One slab has collapsed and when the fog rolls over the mountain, it billows up through the gap like the smoke from a dragon's maw.

Some say that the Drakospito was a very early temple to Hera, for it was on Evia that the goddess was raised and Zeus first noticed her (conveniently forgetting she was his sister). Anticipating her reaction, he tried his usual disguise ploy and turned himself into a little bird, shivering with cold on the mountaintop. She took it to her breast, whereupon Zeus revealed his true form and intentions. "Not on your

life," Hera stamped her foot, "no hanky panky without a wedding." Zeus, young and inexperienced at the time, agreed to matrimony, and prehistoric tribes (the Curetes) initiated rites honoring the holy wedding of Zeus and Hera on Mt. Ohi (Όχη), which continued for hundreds of years. Now comes the question, is the name somehow connected with Hera's emphatic "no" (όχi), the 'i' having been replaced by an 'η' at some point?

The Karystos waterfront abounds with *ouzeris* and cafés in which to ponder this etymological problem. Octopus tentacles dangle from special railings, forming a see-through curtain in front of the sturdy trawlers parked three-deep along the mole. One of the blessings of slow tourist development is that Karystos is still very much of a working-class town where boutiques are far outnumbered by all-purpose emporiums crammed to the roofbeams with old fashioned equipment and appurtenances that might be found in

Southern Evia:
natural park
or wind park?

a folklore museum. Cheese-draining baskets, blue talisman beads for mule bridles, rat-proof cooler cages (*fanaria*) where food was stored in pre-fridge days are just some of the booty on sale. On the first back street parallel to the waterfront, beekeeper Evangelos Hondronastas pours honey mixed with browned sesame seeds onto a marble counter to make crisp, not-too-sweet *pastelli* bars. Garlands of local sausage are looped above pale yellow rounds of *toulomotyri* and *kefalograviera* cheese straight from the sheepfold.

Otto, Greece's first monarch, was so enchanted with the possibilities of Karystos and its huge crescent bay that he dispatched a Bavarian planner to draw up a grid for the new town and even contemplated declaring it his capital. Until his deposition it was called Othonoupolis, and a smattering of neoclassical buildings reminds us of this era.

Antiquities, however, are few. Apart from a fenced-off foundation which may either have belonged to a temple of Apollo or a Roman mausoleum, the only other old stones have been inserted into the walls of the Venetian Bourtzi, the small fort east of the port. The large building opposite it is the Yokalion Foundation, which houses the Archaeological Museum, an impressive 11,000 volume library and a the-

ater where lectures and performances are held regularly. Besides finds from the Dragon House, exhibits include inscriptions, statues and reliefs – notably a delightful one of an aging Hercules reclining on a lion skin with a wine cup under the gaze of a satyr – from the ancient acropolis up at Castello Rosso (*Kokkino Kastro*).

A few more vestiges of the pre-Christian period are to be found in the vicinity of the castle, built by Lombards in 1205. Named after its reddish stones, it was so well designed that the Turks who inherited it from the Venetians withstood four sieges during the Revolution. Below it the pasha created a garden and a citrus grove on the site of Roman baths. Today they belong to the Ktima Montofoli, a very special vineyard producing an elegant, organic dessert wine from grapes dried on the vine, without added alcohol. Pavlos and Marianne Karacostas, who also own the Cellier wineshops in Athens, have transformed the estate which was abandoned in 1950 into a showplace in just 15 years. Besides planting four grape varieties, they have painstakingly restored its Venetian, Turkish and neoclassical ruins with a rare sense of balance and taste. Says Marianne, who was born in Sweden, "Montofoli probably means Mount of Leaves from the Italian *foglie*, but I like to think it means folly. You have to be crazy to work as hard as we have." Myrtoa SA, Karacostas' company, also produces colorful, indispensable sightseers' and walkers' maps of the area, Marianne's marmalade and Myrtilos dry white wine.

After leaving Montofoli, I climbed up to the castle and was nearly blown off by a furious gale. The ancients had a hymn they sang to stop the north wind. I wish we all could learn it. I have a feeling that putting Boreas to rest may be the only way to halt the drive to carve up the mountain and harness him. **O**

Soutnern Evia: natural park or wind park?

Marble columns from Evia stand in Hadrian's Library,
Hagia Sophia in Constantinople and – wait for this – the New
York Public Library.

How to get there

Four ferries per day make the one-hour trip between Rafina and Marmari. From there it is a 20-minute drive to Karystos. Other ferries leave for nearby Stira and Eretria about an hour further north from Agia Marina (beyond Schinias beach) and Oropos. If strong winds keep boats in port, you can always cross over the Halkis bridge at the middle of the island. Rafina ticket agencies, 22940 23150, 26701.

Where to stay

Apollon Suites Hotel (A Class) with its own beach and pool on the eastern outskirts of town, *Karystion* (B Class) near the center, on the edge of a green park overlooking the sea, and *Windmills Studios* (C Class), about 800 m west of town not far from a two km stretch of beach, are all attractive, well-managed bases from which to explore the area. For information and reservations call *Astra Hotels*, 210 9647112-4.

Where to eat

It would be easier to tell you where not to eat, there are so many excellent and atmospheric tavernas both in and outside Karystos. Starting with the waterfront, *Marino's* has good fish and, in season, fresh local asparagus (!), the *Cavo d'Oro* on the first side street west of the main square (look for its yellow chairs) has the best ready-cooked food in town for lunch and serves grills and fries in the evening. *To Kyma*, right on the beach about a kilometer beyond Apollon Suites, and *Anemones* before it are the best bet for fish, though the menu at the former also offers 'lamp' and 'goasts' (sic), while in the hills, *Yeroplatanos* in Myli and *Dimitri's* in Aetos are deservedly the favorites. Both disprove the rule that the better the view the more mediocre the food.

Visits to *Ktima Montofoli* and tastings can be arranged by calling 22240 25951.

Getting around

Nikos Lagounikos at South Evia Tours (SET), 22240 26200, 29010, on the main square, can help with walking trails, kaiki trips, jeep rentals and ferry tickets.

1,3 *Castello Rosso and Mt. Ohi*

2 *Roman columns, Montofoli*

4 *Staircase at Montofoli*

5 *Turkish fountain*

6 *Columns on Mt. Ohi*

7 *Church detail*

8 *Karystos Town Hall*

9 *Drying octopus*

Andros:
still life after the Van Goghs

"The first time I came here," our house guest said, "I kept seeing posters for a Matisse exhibition, but I thought they were advertising an event in Paris. It never occurred to me that paintings of that caliber would be on view on a Greek island."

On the descent we came upon another, even more elegant stone bridge amidst an orange grove and surrounded by rock pools.

W e are walking down the middle of the main street in Andros Town, paved in grey marble flagstones and flanked by sedate neoclassical buildings of pre-Great-War vintage, on our way to this year's exhibition at the Goulandris Museum of Modern Art. It's such an 'un-Cycladic' Hora – quiet, somewhat bourgeois, with just a smattering of tiny *ouzeris*, and not a single kitschy souvenir shop. A new refrigerator is easier to buy than a postcard and the five or six clothing stores display their skirts and bikinis, dozens to a rack outside the door, as if they were running a jumble sale. Clumps of youngsters seem glued to key spots, namely the pavement in front of the *tiropita* shop and the ice cream kiosk; a foreign couple are attempting to put together a picnic from the greengrocer's neatly arranged crates of garden-fresh vegetables; and the cafés in the square shared by the Archaeological Museum and Ottoman fountain are beginning to fill up. But although it is the end of July very few of the passersby are wearing flip-flops and beach garb, nor are there any "Beautiful People" in sight.

In short, this Hora looks more like a small town somewhere in the middle of the Peloponnese than a Cycladic capital renowned for its shipowners and surrounded on three sides by water. Prosperous but not flashy, it is practically unchanged since my first visit in 1972. Despite subtle hints that the New Age is infiltrating – an advertisement for Feng Shui in an occasional shop window, a creperie opened by a young local who's studying Shia-tzu massage – this is still a place where everyone knows everybody else, and the mad nightlife of Mykonos, Paros or Spetses simply does not exist. In fact, Andros is so short on trendy hangouts that were it not for the annual modern art exhibition, the island might not figure on the schedules of half the weekenders who flock to see it every summer.

"How refreshing," our friend had said as we drove from 'our side' – near the Cavo Doro strait separating Andros from Evvia – down the south coast and across to Hora in the middle of the north coast. "It's so undeveloped compared to its neighbors, and so close to Athens."

Refreshing to some, boring to others (especially our teenage grandchildren), most of Andros has a retro atmosphere. There are no organized beaches, no gourmet restaurants, no paragliding and no jet ski rentals. (Which is of course the way we like it.) The roads are poor, power cuts occur

daily and telecommunications are so primitive that it can take days to get online (but we're not complaining; it took us ten years to get our phone). The *meltemi* (insistent summer wind) howls most of the time, driving, stinging sand darts up your nose and into your eyes, overturning your zodiac, until it suddenly drops altogether and the midges attack, biting you below the belt. But there are signs that people are beginning to overlook these idiosyncrasies. Greeks and foreigners alike are buying up plots on windswept hills, bulldozing acres of thyme and heather, drilling for water without permission and throwing their picnic trash into gullies. Construction on the stretch between the port of Gavrion and Batsi, a fishing village turned resort, is giving it a suburban look, and in August cars are parked end-to-end above the long sandy beaches that parallel the road. Most alarming of all are the tasteful signs sprouting on the tracks to deserted headlands, omens of the imminent creation of judges' or bankers' holiday housing projects, which will no doubt be accompanied by a parade of BMWs down to our favorite beaches. Two have already been rendered off-limits by a fish farm and an electricity substation.

What is a person to do but take to the hills. Thanks to a new map published by the Ministry of

the Aegean and the Andros Development Group (for which no address or phone number is listed), even the uninitiated can start to explore this large, mountainous island. The map has a profusion of symbols indicating windmills, pigeon houses, beaches, monasteries and picturesque villages, in addition to hiking trails, for the first time. The mapmakers maintain that they have been cleared and marked; I cannot vouch for this, but if you have hiking experience you can probably find your way and be eminently rewarded for it.

One of the most exciting paths leads from Andros's fourth main town, Korthi (east of Hora), up to the ruins of Faneromeni Castle, and then down through a lush gorge studded with old stone watermills to the village of Sineti. I was introduced to this hike in less than ideal conditions along with a small group from Trekking Hellas. It was mid March, cold as the dickens and snowing. As the six of us set off there were only flurries, but by the time we reached the hamlet of Kochylou, we were caught in a veritable blizzard and took shelter in a general store. It belonged to a vanishing species of shops, usually to be found only in remote mountain villages. Far too big for its wares, its almost bare

Andros:
the Van Goghs

shelves held but a few cans of tomato paste and mackerel, some boxes of cream crackers, rolls of toilet paper and lemon juice in yellow plastic bottles, plus a few chairs. Lucky for us, the owner was happy to brew up some sage tea. This thawed our bones somewhat, though the room was so frosty that wisps of our conversation lingered in puffs around our heads. When the snowstorm finally relented, we trudged up the mountain to the castle with the wind squeezing tears from our eyes and sandpapering our cheeks and noses. As we reached the blustery top, fearful of being yanked into the Aegean, we had that hale and hearty feeling that comes from battling the elements.

This soon vanished with the heavy drizzle that followed us along the river and we did not pay proper attention to the lovely water mills as we staggered down the cobbled *kalderimi*, but as with most ordeals, we were so relieved when it was over and we had reached the cozy café in Sineti, that our feat soon took on heroic proportions.

Prosperous but not flashy, the Hora is practically unchanged since my first visit in 1972.

The next day was sunny and mild and we climbed from Aladino near Hora (you'll find it on the map) down to a charming stone bridge and up, endlessly up, to the 10th century Panachrantos Monastery, where the sole monk, the abbot, who had been snowbound for several days, concocted a superb *makaronada* with tomato sauce and sat us down to a winey, gossipy lunch. On the descent we came upon another, even more elegant stone bridge amidst an orange grove and surrounded by rock pools. It was not a long walk back along the road to the Hora, the Egli Hotel and a siesta before dinner.

Our final trek started from Strapouries, a village strung out among the cypresses, olive groves and gushing streams just southwest of Hora, where you'll find one of the island's best tavernas, Pertesis. We climbed above the timber line and the last dry-stone-wall into pastures napped in deep snow. The sky could not have been bluer, the air clearer. We stripped to our shirts and plunged our boots into the blurred footprints left by our guide a few days earlier. Drunk on the magnificent view, we leapt about the ridge like goats, picnicked on a dry boulder, and swapped life stories. It's true that occasionally we did pause to wring out our socks, but that was merely a trifling inconvenience. All was glorious until we reached the cliffs above Palaiopoli and there the path and footprints abruptly ended.

Andros:
still life after
the Van Goghs

What to do? We descended, following the electricity pylons, grabbing hold of oleander bushes, slithering between rocks, knees shaking, toes turning blue, wishing we could simply tumble down the waterfall to our left. Eventually we made it back to the road, though if we'd had the map we'd have seen that the trail winds all the way down to Batsi.

If my exertions leave you resolved never to leave the safety of your car except to lounge on a sandy beach, you can still get some idea of the interior of Andros from the main road. As you will have gathered, it's greener than most Aegean islands and even exports its Sariza spring water to the mainland. Its architecture ranges from three-story mansions owned by families with Venetian names and surrounded by cypress woods, giant plane trees and citrus groves to brown stone farmhouses owned by families with Albanian names and flanked by threshing floors, shaggy sheep the color of the dry shrubs and olive trees that have bent like old crones to escape the wind. The terracing of centuries past sculpts the hills and mountainsides, while the slopes are sliced into erratic shapes by handsome walls of slate panels set erect between smaller stones and stepped donkey tracks. Between them stand white dovecotes, Byzantine churches and countless flat-roofed chapels, monuments of a time when the countryside supported far more people than it does today.

So by all means, do visit Andros. It's the only island in Greece where you can see world-class modern art before you climb a 900-meter mountain. Be sure to take a look at the Goulandris permanent sculpture collection and the annual retrospectives of contemporary Greek artists at the Petros & Marika Kydoniefs Foundation, before you set off to explore. But please don't come back and build a villa. ●

How to get there

There are four ferries daily from Rafina to Andros; Port Police tel. 22940 22300. You cannot get to the island from Piraeus.

Where to stay

Most of the island's hotels and rooms are in Batsi, but there are several attractive bungalow complexes on the outskirts of Gavrion, such as *Aktio* (tel. 22820 71607), and more luxurious surroundings can be found at the *Andros Holiday Hotel* (Gavrion, tel. 22820 71097), *Perrakis Hotel* (Kipri beach, tel. 22820 71456) and *Paradise Hotel* (near Hora, tel. 22820 22187).

Where to eat

In Hora, there are several tavernas along the waterfront west of the stairs next to the art museums. Our favorite taverna in Batsi is *Stamatis*, up the stairs above the port/parking lot; and in Gavrion *Vengera* has a imaginative menu and pleasant location protected from the meltemi.

1 *Andros Town*
2 *Tis Grias to Pidima beach*
3 *View from Faneromeni Castle*
4 *Typical view*
5 *Sunset*
6 *On the north coast*

Andros:
a walk on the wilder side

When J. Theodore Bent and his wife traveled around the Cyclades in the 1880s, his impressions of Andros were colored by the foul March weather and the prevalence of "obnoxious animalculae," aka, fleas and bedbugs. Nevertheless, able to speak Greek, he enjoyed himself in the eastern half which he found almost paradisaical with its "delicious streams," fertile valleys and "lofty towers." Gavrion, the present port, was a different story. "Of all places in the world Gavrion is one of the most desolate… The inhabitants of Gavrion, too, struck us as morose, and not too hospitably inclined." He does admit, however, that part of the problem was his inability to communicate with them. They spoke no Greek.

Andros is alone among the Cyclades in that a large portion of its population is of Albanian stock. These 'Arvanites' arrived in the early 15th century.

A ndros is alone among the Cyclades in that a large portion of its population is of Albanian stock. They are the descendants of mercenaries who were brought in by the Venetians in the early 15th century to defend the island against Turks and pirates and given the whole of western Andros to cultivate in return. The men and women whom Bent met had not been hellenized even after almost five hundred years. They had kept their own dress, customs and language, and had remarkably little contact with the more prosperous families of Greek and Italian origin in the valleys around Hora, cut off as they were by high rugged mountains and barren, windswept headlands. But today's *Arvanites*, which is how they are called to distinguish them from modern Albanians, are 100 percent Greek. Only a handful of the older generation speak *Arvanitika*, and many of the younger ones have no idea of their heritage.

Yiannis Rerras, a beekeeper in Gavrion with a keen interest in history, maintains that the tribes who first settled in Illyria, present-day Albania, were in fact Greek. As proof, he points to the existence in the *Arvanitika* dialect of many words whose roots are identical to those used by Homer. He suggests that the language and identity changed over the centuries with the influx of Slavs. He also suggests that the tendency of the 'real Greek' ruling classes to regard the *Arvanites* as second class citizens, despite their enormous contribution to the War of Independence, was responsible for the gradual disappearance of their language and traditions. "The people were illiterate but they wanted to get ahead, so they suppressed the things that made them different."

Two factors speeded up their assimilation. The Hora Andriots, who had a knack for trade, were so quick to turn their sailing ships into steamers that the island's merchant navy became one of the largest in the world. The *Arvaniti* farm boys they recruited as crew adapted themselves to the sea almost as quickly; soon, too, their Greek lost its distinctive accent. At the same time, up until the Second World War, Arvaniti women were also travelling abroad, learning new ways as wet nurses for upperclass mothers in Athens, Asia Minor and Egypt. They brought back so many jewels that their husbands decided to take it easy and acquired a reputation for being lazy.

Then came the German Occupation. Says Eleni Mamai, who has a waterfront *psilikatsidiko* selling

everything from swimming fins to schoolbooks, "That was when the rich people in Hora stopped treating us as peasants. The farmers were not hungry, they had their crops, and the others came crawling to them like starved cats – with their silver." Eleni's family in Varidi near the northwest coast had an oil press and fruit trees. "We had a couple from Hora living with us, doing carpentry and housework in exchange for food. Once they gave us a grammophone and records in exchange for a chicken."

Thodoros Helmis, proud owner of a thousand olive trees and a new state-of-the-art Italian oil press, also in Varidi, paints a different picture. "Sure, when they needed us they were nice, but after the war many *Horiani* accused us of stealing from them and sued us to get back their belongings!"

Whatever the disagreements, the *Arvanitohoria* or villages in the northwest and center of Andros are now deserted or semi-abandoned. A visitor driving through on the way to a splendid beach will barely notice that the scrub-tufted hills are crisscrossed with mulepaths, terracing and meandering walls. Closer inspection reveals dozens of ruins in the same grey-brown stone: sheepfolds, threshing floors, dovecotes and *konakia* – huts that sheltered farmers, flocks and wine presses at some distance from the house proper. These huts are primitive; in fact, they are surprisingly similar to the Geometric-era models in the Hora Archaeological Museum, but their niches and shelves, troughs, ovens and fireplaces show a wonderful synthesis of form and function. Poke around these houses and your appreciation for our own comforts soars.

Curiously, the *Arvaniti* villages are very spread out. Unlike the typical Greek pattern of houses clustered round a square with a church, café and fountain, in Andros even the family homes stand apart from one another, and there is no word for *plateia* (square) in *Arvanitika*. Was there no community feeling? Yannis Rerras says, "On the contrary, but friends would gather at homes, especially in winter, sit round the fire, tell stories and pass the *tsipouro*."

Until the 1960s, this outback was densely populated. There were two schools in Makrotandalo (northwest Andros), each with 70 pupils; every ribbon of land was cultivated; every village had at least one olive press. Thodoros Helmis remembers packing his donkeys with oil, flour and vegetables for the three-hour trek to Gavrion, where there were a few rudimentary shops, and then back again, twice a week. Ironically, once roads were laid, whole families used them to pack up and leave for Athens and North America, so that only the old remain.

Andros:
a walk on the
wilder side

Andreas Katsikis lives by himself in the ghost village of Agios Symeon, miles from anywhere except a holiday settlement yet to be built on a beach only a jeep can get to. He shrugs off the loneliness. His sons visit every day, he says, though he wouldn't mind a Romanian woman to keep house for him. What really worries him is his dry well.

You hear the same complaint wherever you go this summer. After a series of rainless winters, even the island once known as Hydrousa (Watery) is running low on water. Nevertheless, there is still more water here than on most Aegean islands. Sariza continues to export bottles of the stuff to the mainland, and the area around Hora is as green as the Riviera. Emerald valleys and ravines choked with plane trees are a common sight even in the bleaker western half. Ami, the biggest of all the *Arvanitohoria* high up the slopes of Mt. Petalon, could be in Pelion it boasts so many fruit trees, chestnuts, walnuts and, in spring, rare wild peonies and primroses. On a blistering August day it can be chilly, cloaked in mist. But you no longer hear

the prattle of a brook amidst the rustling leaves, and underground springs have shrunk to a trickle.

The Andros of the *Arvanites* has few sights for the average tourist, but it does have the island's best beaches. On the south coast between Gavrion and Batsi – the fishing village turned resort – sandy strands run parallel to the road and are rarely buffeted by the legendary Andros *meltemi*. Cross the mountains to the north side and the beaches are even more beautiful, fed (sometimes) by reed-banked rivers. At Zorkos and Vitali, farmers have opened tavernas where they serve home-grown vegetables, creamy local cheese and lambchops from their own flocks, with not a plastic chair on the premises. On a mild winter weekend, the attraction could be exploring ravines sprinkled with old watermills or hiking across heather-filled hills between villages.

Andros has been slow to catch on to tourism. The sea captains and shipowners discouraged development in their sector, but 'permitted' it in Batsi, which has tripled in size in the past twenty years. Rooms, studio apartments and impressive villas are burgeoning on the parched hillsides between Batsi and Gavrion, to accommodate the new demand for a home-away-from-home just two hours from Rafina. Even Gavrion is no longer desolate, though it would never win a beauty contest. But what about the Andriots? Are the *Arvanites* still as morose and inhospitable as Bent and some subsequent visitors have found them?

I asked Yannis Rerras, who smiled broadly beneath his magnificent

Andros:
a walk on the
wilder side

Farmers have opened tavernas where they serve home-grown vegetables, creamy local cheese and lambchops, with not a plastic chair in sight.

white mustache. "People might find us a bit stern. But we are fair, we don't play games and we have *besa* – we keep our word" (though this does not necessarily apply to plumbers and electricians!). Thodoros Helmis and his wife Theodora plied us with *tsipouro*, melon and sweets, regaling us with tales of out-witting the Italians during the war before we could even approach the subject of buying oil, and sent us away with kilos of tomatoes and more melons free of charge. As for Eleni Mamai, you couldn't accuse her of being inhospitable. She was one of the few to welcome the second wave of Albanian immigrants when they descended on the island in droves ten years ago. She had picked up *Arvanitika* as a girl, despite her grandparents' disapproval, and although the languages are quite different now they can converse as easily as Swedes and Danes. "I took pity on them," she told me, perhaps remembering snubs in years past, "when the people of Hora would close the door in our faces if we asked for a drink of water."

Finally I asked Tom Rowe, an American screenwriter who has had a house near Fellos for 30 years. "Unpleasant, morose, inhospitable? In all my days here, I've never seen anything but the good, kind side of these people. Give them a smile and see where the frowns go." ○

How to get there

There are ferries morning and afternoon from Rafina to Andros; Port Police tel. 22940 22300, and the trip takes two hours. You cannot get to the island from Piraeus.

Where to stay

Most of the island's hotels and rooms in Batsi are closed in winter but the *Ostria* bungalow complex (tel. 22820 71551-3) on the outskirts of Gavrion, the *Blue Bay Hotel* on the coast south of Batsi (tel. 22820 41150), and the modest *Galaxias Hotel* (tel. 22820 71249-50) on the Gavrion waterfront all remain open.

Where to eat

Besides the tavernas recommended on page 199, try *Balkoni tou Aigaiou* on a cliff overlooking the horizon at Ano Aprovato (6 km from Batsi), *Belalis* at Kato Aprovato on the main road, and *Yannoulis* opposite Agios Petros beach.

11

1,5 *Ammolochos*
2 *Typical view with path*
3 *Zorkos beach*
4 *Andreas Katsikis*
6 *Ruined hut*
7 *Fountain house*
8 *Arni*
9 *Terraced hillside in spring*
10 *Old bridge*
11 *Thodoros Helmis*

Tinos with the pilgrims

"You should go to Tinos on the 15th of August. The crowds are mostly Gypsies and Filipinos, the Greeks make the pilgrimage 9 days later."

This statement floated by a Greek friend one July evening in Andros piqued my curiosity. Could it be true? What was this all about? I resolved to find out. Tinos is just a 90-minute ferry ride from Andros so it would be easy to go in the morning and return in the afternoon. But would two and a half hours there be enough? The ticket agent rolled his eyes, "More than enough."

Church bells clanged, cannons fired salutes, and every ship's horn sent prolonged blasts up to the skies. All of Tinos was doing its best to squeeze into the square on the 15th of August.

The 10 am ferry was practically empty, all the faithful having arrived the day before, and we approached the port to an eruption of noise. Church bells clanged, cannons fired salutes, and every ship's horn in the harbor sent prolonged blasts up to the skies. All of Tinos was doing its best to squeeze into the square nearest the harbor, while more people hung out of surrounding balconies, roof terraces and window ledges. The area around the dignitaries' platform was impenetrable, but even as we threaded our way through the back alleys we could hear the unmistakable tones over the loudspeaker of Greece's favorite personality, the Archbishop of Athens. "When you threaten the Greeks' freedom or their religion, they become lions." The crowd roared back its approval.

By this time we had joined the throng and it was plain to see that this was no gathering of immigrants. Gypsies there were, to be sure; the women dressed in shimmering golds, pinks and purples, the men in clean shirts and trousers. Their bedding, blankets rolled into balls as large as Sisyphus's boulder, lay stuffed into corners, forming cushions for sprawling kids. But we saw few foreigners as we elbowed

Greeks in their Sunday finery for a glimpse of the platform. On one side of the rostrum, New Democracy leader Costas Karamanlis's sun-tanned cheeks and his wife's blonde hair gleamed under the noonday sun, while the local politicos and bravos sweated patiently in coats and ties. On the other stood the amassed clergy – lesser priests swathed in black, the hierarchy in resplendent robes of ivory and gold, with globelike golden crowns. Christodoulos himself was hidden from view, but when he finally gave up the microphone, the crowd awarded him another ovation and then began to straggle away. Papoutsis, the minister for the merchant

marine, took his place and began to talk about the Italian sinking of the 'Elli' on August 15, 1940 to a dwindling audience. They'd heard it all before.

We too wandered off in the direction of a bakery with promising smells and 'real' old-fashioned bread, but the sounds of the band starting up pulled us back to Megalohari Avenue, the wide street that connects the port with the Evangelistria church. The dignitaries were parading the famous icon back inside. The band marched by in their smart white uniforms, followed by the acolytes and their 'shepherd,' a man no taller than most of the boys who scurried alongside, hissing fierce instructions to keep them in line. Then came the lesser priests, with faces as somber as their robes; the icon invisible inside its silver palanquin; and the bishops with Christodoulos in the center, his arms raised in triumphal greeting, smiling broadly at the ripple of applause that accompanied his passage. A few paces behind, Karamanlis also grinned at his (fewer) clapping supporters. There were no other smiles in the whole procession. Must have been the heat.

This street is a kitsch collector's paradise, offering up sculptures, handbags, plastic toys and ingenious reproductions of the Virgin.

We waited until the street was empty to continue up the avenue. Three women in long pants were making painful progress on all fours up the stained brown carpet provided for this pious act. One slumped on the curb and took deep drags from a cigarette to restore her will. They attracted so little attention that shoppers stocking up on Turkish delight, souvenirs and javelin-sized candles missed their fingertips by inches. By now most of the pedestrians were Gypsies, cheerful clusters who obligingly posed for our cameras. "Send the pictures to us in Sparti, Lakonias," they cried, "The postmen know us. You don't need our names."

We didn't enter the main church – the crush was too great, the air too thick with incense. I didn't even light a candle, preferring the dusky solitude of a country chapel for my devotions to this, garish to me, assembly line. We descended the other street to the port instead, and this is where we saw the foreigners: Africans selling wooden sculptures, handbags, plastic toys and silk shirts, as they do at any city open-air

Tinos with the pilgrims

market. This street is a kitsch collector's paradise and one wonders what the Virgin would think of the ingenious ways her image has been reproduced to make money.

Our remaining hour was spent having an exceptionally bad lunch at a taverna we'd remembered as good. No doubt the holiday pressure was to blame because it's hard to find bad cooking on this island of gastronomic artistry.

Back on the waterfront we hurried to the dock, where hundreds of people had already been herded under sheds until they could be boarded. In the course of our long wait I heard someone mutter, "The moment people put on a uniform they become stupid and disorganized." But at least the ship itself was comfortable. The Gypsies spread their blankets in any available space and made themselves at home, a group of women in their sixties sang and chattered throughout the journey, other passengers played cards, and most eventually dozed off. One Gypsy clan attracted my attention, they were so numerous and so handsome. The chain-smoking, topaz-eyed grandfather answered my questions with humor and grace, even inserting a few words of English. "Why do we come to Tinos? It's a tradition. I've come every year for the past forty years. We are all Christian Orthodox. We come for the Virgin, she does us good. But it doesn't matter whether you're a Muslim, Protestant or Jewish. There's one God looking after us all. I wish you and whoever you love well."

Then I spotted a lone, sweet-looking woman reading a prayer book. She told me that she'd arrived in Tinos at 10 pm the previous evening and spent the whole night praying in church. She'd been awake for well over 24 hours, but the crowds and the bother (*talaiporeia*) were of no importance. She dismissed them, saying "The Virgin gives me strength." I told her how impressed I was by the great variety of people making this pilgrimage and we talked about the role of the Church in the history of the Greek nation. She said, "Orthodoxy and Greekness are synonymous." "But can you not be a Catholic Greek and or a Jewish Greek?" I asked.

"I won't say yes, and I won't say no," came the ambiguous reply.

"What about the Gypsies? They are Orthodox, too".

She closed her eyes and shook her head. "Oh, no, they are different," she said and walked away.

Tinos, August 15

The other Tinos

When a place is very famous for something – the way Tinos is famous for being the Lourdes of Greece – any other attributes it may have tend to be overshadowed. And when an island is said to attract crowds of a certain type of person – be they pious pilgrims, flamboyant gays or back-packing hash-heads as in the case of Tinos, Mykonos and Ios – you think twice about what sort of appeal that island might have for you as an agnostic, straight, wine drinker. Just squeezing onto a ferry with all those gospel-reading maiden aunts and flouncing gypsies bound for Tinos on the 15th of August is enough to quell any glimmer of curiosity about what else might go on there.

Despite the port's intimate connection with things sacred, religion has not dampened the nightlife there.

N evertheless, fed up with trying to turn our patch of thistles in Andros into a garden, we'd popped over to Tinos for the day four summers ago. A mini-tour of some quintessentially Cycladic villages with a friendly taxi driver and a better than average lunch in town were enough to keep a vague notion of revisiting the island percolating in the back of our minds ever since. So when a friend who knows Tinos well proposed a walking expedition to mitigate the excesses of Easter, we accepted with alacrity. The weather should be perfect, the priests hoarse, the tourists still in northern Europe… what better moment?

To save time we took the morning Sea Jet from Gavrion (one hour's ride to Tinos, two from Rafina), and by 11:30 we were contemplating the many steps up to the ruined Venetian fortress at Xobourgo, the island's second highest peak. Xobourgo, or 'outside the town', was the chief settlement during the Geometric/Archaic period and the Venetian occupation, whereas in Classical, Roman and Byzantine times the *bourgo* proper was around the port, as it is today. It is up here at Xinara, just below the ruins, that the Catholic bishop has his seat, a living relic of 500 years of Italian rule. Ironically, given the island's fame as an Orthodox shrine, one in three Tiniots is Catholic. The competition must be responsible for its extravagant number of churches – some 750 in all. And as we were to see, they come in all types and sizes: with elegant, sculpted campaniles right out of the Veneto or silver Byzantine domes, bright blue turrets like large doorknobs or flat Cycladic roofs, gar-landed baroque exteriors or facades studded with ancient columns, bas reliefs of the double-headed eagle or niches holding full statues of the Virgin.

"Hold on to something as you round the corners," said our guide. "The wind tends to be really fierce up here." You'd have thought Aeolus himself was trying to dislodge us from his realm, though strictly speaking the ancients placed his abode on Tinos's other peak, Mt. Tsinia, which at 725 m is about 150 m higher than Xobourgo. Which just goes to show that weather patterns have not changed very much in the last several thousand years.

Sections of crumbling wall and some barrel-vaulted tunnels are all that's left of the castle, erected by the Venetians in the late 14th century. There is little to evoke the days when "Tinos [was] the richest and most populous of all the Aegean islands… with the exception of Chios." The Venetian official who wrote this comment in 1563 on the eve of the Turkish conquest of the Cyclades went on to report that "the fortress is almost impregnable, though the garrison consists of but twelve foot soldiers; the population is 9000, a good part of whom speak Italian and are Catholics. Such is their civilisation, that this remote island scarcely differs at all from Venetia." Though all the other Aegean islands fell, Tinos remained Venetian until 1715. It might have held out longer for the fortress was indeed well built and the Greek population equipped with determination and plenty of supplies for a long siege. The Venetian commander, however, surrendered with barely a shot fired and sailed back home unremorseful. To their credit, his superiors sen-

tenced him to life imprisonment for taking bribes and rewarded his officers by dousing them with molten silver; the Greek defenders are said to have been shipped to slavery in Africa.

By and large, however, the Turks dealt kindly with Tinos, extending the commercial privileges enjoyed under the Venetians and the Byzantines before them, and keeping their presence to a minimum of one or two officials. They allowed them self-rule, though you can be sure the tax collector would have been a frequent visitor.

Was it this benign neglect that has made the Tinians so artistic, tidy, polite and hospitable? As we followed the cobbled paths from Xobourgo to the pretty village of Ktikados and then down to the sea at Kionia, about half an hour's stroll from the port, it struck me that while Tinos certainly has attractive scenery, for once the man-made component is what delights the eye: the fields and slopes dotted with

Tinos's signature dovecote-towers that remind me of the open-work embroidered curtains that hang in so many island windows; the dozens of villages with their newly whitewashed steps, homes and chapels;, squares dappled by plane trees and framed by tomato-red geraniums; fountain-houses where women still scrub their laundry while gossiping with friends and, above almost every doorway, whether modern or traditional, a fanlight carved from local marble. This is a place that seems to have spawned half the artists in the National Gallery and where even the sliced apples in a taverna will have slender strips of shiny peel left as decoration.

Back in town, in a park below the cathedral, the busts of Tinos's six most famous sculptors and painters stand like the sages, at a discreet remove from the processional way up to the church. Halepas, Philippotis, Gyzis and Lytras, the best known, were following a profession begun with Pheidias's father and maybe earlier.

On this April evening no penitents are crawling up the dingy carpet that runs from the waterfront to the Evangelistria and there are only a few cus-

The other
Tinos

tomers rummaging through the bins overflowing with plastic flagons for holy water, 2-meter-long candles, cheap icons, and tin *ex votos* stamped with a leg, an eye, an infant, an ear for the afflicted to offer to the Virgin. Sandwiched among these religious knicknacks are some classy antiques shops and stalls piled high with Turkish delight, nougat and *pastelli* – to sweeten the disappointment if no miracle transpires? But miracles have been happening ever since a young nun named Pelagia dreamed of the icon waiting to be discovered near the ruins of a temple dedicated, incongruously, to Dionysos. The event coincided nicely with the country's revolt against the Ottomans, stamping the insurrection with divine approval while securing renown for Tinos. There seems to be some disagreement about the precise date of Pelagia's revelation, ranging from 1822 to 1833, but 1823 has the most votes.

Maybe there is something in the Tinos breezes that is conducive to good health, because pilgrims flocked to the sanctuary of Poseidon and Amphitrite at Kionia from the Classical period until the

4th century AD, the men seeking cures from the 'Great Doctor,' the women appealing to his wife for an end to their infertility, before crossing the channel to the holy island of Delos. Poseidon is also credited with sending storks to rid Tinos, then known as Ophiousa or 'snake-ridden', of its serpents. The lone viper we saw perhaps indicates the need for more burnt offerings to the god.

Despite the port's intimate connection with things sacred, religion has not dampened nightlife in Pallada, the old section of town, where beautiful houses and shops have been converted into *ouzeris*, tavernas and bars. Exposed arches, niches, painted neoclassical ceilings, and

Tinian carved plaques and fanlights decorate even the smallest dive in Club Alley, where dancing on the table tops after midnight is a commonplace. The same preoccupation with delicate touches shows up in the cooking. In a real find called the Koutouki, local specialties like wild fennel fritters, sautéed sun-dried tomatoes, grilled wild mushrooms, anchovies marinated in lemon juice and garlic, *kopanisti* (piquant soft cheese), and spicy liver with peppers and onions had us all ecstatic – the *loukoumades* devoured at tea time having in no way dented our appetites.

Obviously, we'd forgotten that one of the reasons for our walk was to shed some of Easter's extra kilos.

So the next day we vowed restraint, a vow that was broken right after breakfast when an elderly couple in our first village, Kechros, invited us into their cellar for a glimpse of their collection of the family's traditional farm and kitchen tools accompanied by a shot of *raki* and some delectable sweet cheese pies. Thus fortified we marched on, cutting a swathe around the so-called Kechrovounia to the next two magical villages, Duo Horia (twins) and Triantaros. Here we succumbed to the marble work of Yiannis Kyrarinis, one of the few craftsmen not located in the northwest village of Pyrgos where there is

a fine arts school near the marble quarries. We arranged for our fanlights to be delivered to our pension and went on towards the coast, passing bare hillsides etched with terraces and sea-buffeted rocks. Over lunch at Porto, a new resort, we planned the next day's excursion to Pyrgos, the valley of the dovecotes, the portlet of Panorama, and perhaps a detour to Volax, a village surrounded by boulders strewn helter-skelter like giant cannonballs. But torrential rains on Saturday morning saw us scurrying for the 9 am ferry back to Andros and the comforts of home, promising ourselves we'd be back. It's wonderful to have an island like the other Tinos on our doorstep. ◯

Private guided walks can be arranged by John and Annie Apgar. For information call 210 8950527.

How to get there
Boats leave Piraeus and Rafina several times a day for Tinos, while the Sea Jet Catamaran from Rafina shaves the time in half.

Where to stay
Hotel *Tinion*, B class, in one of the grand old houses of Tinos, next to the post office. An extra perk is the splendid breakfast. Tel: 22830 22261, fax 22830 24754.
Hotel *Leandros*, C class, attractive island-style architecture and furnishings in a handy location, charming owner. Tel. 22830 23545, 24390.

Where to eat
Koutouki, in an alley off the waterfront, for wonderful Tinian specialities; *Drossia*, in Ktikados, with delicious little cheese pies, *keftedes* and robust rabbit *stifado*; *Antonis*, at Porto, said to have the best moussaka in the Cyclades.

10

1 *Old stone bridge*
2 *Dovecote*
3 *Walkers*
4 *Typical view*
5 *Xobourgo and chapel*
6 *Tinian relief sculpture*
7 *Hillside with dovecotes*
8 *Dovecote*
9 *Xinara and Venetian castle*
10 *Typical village square*

The faint-hearted hiker's guide to Kea

The offer of a friend's house in Kea came as we were sifting through possibilities for a respite from the evening news. Right in the middle of the Hora, with a jasmine-scented balcony and view of the sun setting over Attica, it sounded romantic, quaint and well out of range of "Big Brother" and appalling news broadcasts. So, armed with both hand-drawn and computer-drafted maps and a loving description of how to treat the plumbing and the potted plants, we drove off the ferry and up the hill in the direction of Kea's main village.

Kea was a major center of the Cycladic civilization and in the early days of steamships, an important fuelling station for the eastern Mediterranean.

The road snaked higher and higher, past little oases of beans and tomatoes, amongst bare terraces stacked with boxy beehives, without seeming to bring us any nearer to the Hora, which indeed we didn't even glimpse until we were about to enter it. Such was the genius of the original town planners in hiding from the pirates' gaze. There has been a settlement in this spot since the 7th century BC: Ioulis, one of the four in the historic Tetrapolis of Keos, and the only one to survive past antiquity. Korissia or Livadia, the port, was not continuously inhabited.

We left the car in the lower parking area as instructed and began the climb up to the house, jauntily at first, past the first square and its taxi stand, through an archway to a second, elongated, square lined with cafés, tavernas, the archaeological museum "closed for repairs," and a few neoclassical buildings. Then, checking each turn against the map, we ticked off landmarks – a decidedly unsuper market, a more promising pastry shop, a shoe store, a gift shop – trudging ever more slowly. Where was this hideaway? Up some steps, under another arch, and finally the little black iron gate of the house itself opening onto a flight of the steepest steps I've ever hoisted myself up, the *coup de grâce.*

We'd arrived, and yes it was adorable, but so squeezed by adjoining buildings that the amazing view could only be enjoyed by ascending to the roof, via another excruciating staircase. We collapsed onto the fourposter bed, hoping to gain enough strength to go down to the port for dinner and then back up again. Over the course of our stay, we discovered the Hora's upper parking area, which meant we could juggle our ascents and descents to the car/house according to our energy level, but there never was that longed-for 'camel's way,' gently, monotonously flat.

One advantage of living in a town closed off to traffic is that you are not plagued by honking horns or the unmufflered passage of souped-up motorbikes, the scourge of many a picturesque port. On the other hand, the chatter on the street below resonates alarmingly in your dreams, and the church bells and Sunday carillon make you wish you'd resisted that last carafe of *krasi*.

The biggest plus to our location was its proximity to the path (a gentle one, at last) that leads to Kea's most famous monument, the Archaic Lion, a splendidly whiskered feline wearing the faintest of smiles. No fearsome predator this fellow, he is carved with elegant economy from the rock on which he reclines. I had seen him once before, almost thirty years ago, near the end of a wonderful morning's walk from the Kastriani Monastery, at the northeast tip of the island, to Hora.

Then we had spent the night in the monastery's spartan guest quarters, had a frugal breakfast and looked longily at the pristine coves flanking it hundreds of sheer feet below, before setting out across the hills. In those days the path was evident but not clearly marked; today attractive burnt-wood signs pepper the island, pointing the way and approximate times to beaches, villages and ancient sites, making Kea a treat for walkers in any season.

As we drove along the coast and up to the monastery, a pilgrimage that attracts many first-time visitors whether for the view or more pious reasons, I saw how much the island has changed. So many fancy yachts were parked at Vourkari, a large protected bay north of the port, it looked like a mini Zea marina. Every other car was a mighty 4x4 and peasant houses were nonexistent among the new villas constructed of the ubiquitous grey local stone. It was obvious that all the Albanians we'd noticed in the Hora were gainfully employed, being masters of the vanishing art of stone masonry. As for the Athenian weekenders, they made mockery of a recent report that 60 percent of Greeks subsist below the poverty line.

Across the bay, surrounding a chapel dedicated to Agia Irini, are the ruins left by much earlier residents in the 3rd and 2nd millennium BC, when Kea was a major center of the Cycladic civilization. The rather impressive fortification walls differ little from those encircling the gardens erected just a few years ago. Further on an abandoned 19th century coal warehouse is an unlikely reminder that in the early days of steamships, Kea was an important fuelling station for the eastern Mediterranean. In fact my guidebook says that hundreds of people worked there and in the enamel factory, whose solitary smokestack throws an unexpected exclamation point into the collection of low buildings behind the port.

The book, *Kea*, a pretty edition appallingly translated, is full of startling information, depicting a society unimaginable on this Aegean outpost, were of aristocrats with Venetian pedigrees served as consuls

to every major European nation, overseeing a bustling trade in red wine, barley, silk, waterproof goat-hair overcoats, and acorns by the ton. These last were bound for the tanneries of Syros and are no longer a viable product. But the oak forests exist, another unusual sight in a part of the world where the olive reigns supreme.

They grow in several parts of the island, on terraces carving every possible inch of hillside into manageable plots. There are pockets of wheat stubble, vineyards, olives to be sure, and pasture (for surprisingly athletic cows), but oak trees are the most prevalent plants and the western flank, where they are most common, is also the gentlest, most beautiful part of Kea.

The chic new resorts, Pisses and Koundouros, face Attica. Pisses, at the end of a green valley glowing with bright red pomegranates, was the site of another of the ancient cities, Poiessa. The surrounding mountainsides are supposedly littered with walls and temple foundations from that era, but we only stopped to inspect a marble medieval fountain and a Classical watchtower tilting crazily over a crimson-domed church. In

The real allure of Kea lies inland.

Koundouros, the passion for stone villas has outdone itself. The hills around the beach, which twenty years ago were empty, have been turned into a Munchkin land of fake windmills, 'authentic' down to their thatched roofs, and luxury hotel-bungalow complexes. The old Xenia hotel, a yellow monstrosity on stilts, is said to have housed the Colonels who were exiled here until the new government decided what to do with them. A venerable local we met tut-tutted at all the development, "Vouliagmeni today, Faliron tomorrow," he said, rolling his eyes.

For me, the real allure of Kea lies inland, especially now that the swimming season has all but ended. Here there are no colonies of summer residents, just wooded hills, centuries-old farm houses, chapels built with ancient remnants, and a major ancient site, Karthaia, the fourth city in the Tetrapolis. Friends had said it was a must, the guidebook is filled with praise and photos to back it up. We followed the road signs as far as the path, took a deep breath and set off. The old boy had said it would take "20 minutes or so," the hikers' arrow 40. The 4-kilometer descent was knee-tremblingly steep down an uneven mule track, but shaded for the most part. Somewhere beyond the point of no return we questioned the wisdom of our trek but stubbornly pushed on. One hour later, we pushed through a reed-brake onto a beach. Where were the ruins?

Beet-red and panting like an overworked hound, I plunged into the sea and swam beyond the point, where I could see a couple of people scrambling up the promontory. There seemed to be a column or two and above them, higher still, a little white church. Drat,

4

so unfair; I felt like shredding the guidebook. All those pictures taken at sunset, in springtime, flowers and green fields instead of parched hillsides seen through the sweat of high noon, and no mention that you had to climb another mountain to reach your destination. Fed up but resolutely determined, and revived by the swim, I picked my way up to the first plateau where the foundations of a temple to Athena lay. But no further; Apollo's temple and other wonders on the probably even more photogenic upper summit were simply out of reach that day.

Back down on the beach, I rejoined my husband who was reclining under the portico of a little chapel. We mustered our dwindling will to walk, having given up hope that a kaiki was going to come to the rescue, and started up the path. Miraculously, we managed the ascent in the same amount of time as the descent and sank into the soft seats of the car.

The road to Hora took us past Kato Meria where we spied a taverna, the only one in this area. The locals there looked at us with awe, "You're heroes to do that walk. But you could have taken the shorter path from Agios Nikolaos, which comes out on top of the site." Now they tell us. But a few bottles of beer, a delicious salad, fresh laid eggs and real fried potatoes combined with their friendly conversation restored us. And we thought to ourselves, "how lucky we were to have had that little house in the middle of Hora to get us fit for our hiking exploits." From now on that little promenade would be a piece of cake, and maybe next time we'll take the old cobbled path from Hora all the way to Karthaia. ○

5

How to get there

Kea is only an hour's boat ride from Lavrion but the schedule is erratic and often disrupted by the hint of strong winds. Call the port police (22920 25249) before you set out. If you take a car, you'll need to reserve ahead (Lavrion agent, 22920 26777; Kea agent, 22880 21313). NEL (210 4223185) and Minoan Lines (210 4199000) serve Kea from Piraeus.

Where to stay

There are a few hotels open all year, including *Karthaia* (22880 21204) and *I Tzia Mas* (21305) in Korissia, the port, and *Ioulis* in the Kastro district of Hora (22177). The Stegadi travel bureau will also help you find a room (21435). And there is always the *Kastriani monastery hostel* (21348).

Where to eat

In Korissia, *I Akri* has excellent meat and wonderful red wine; *I Strofi tou Mimi* at the far end of Vourkari where the road turns for Otzia is a highly recommended *ouzeri*; *Orlando's* is another good *ouzeri* in Hora; and the *tavernaki with no name* in Kato Meria saved our lives after the walk to Karthaia and back. If you have a sweet tooth, don't leave the island without stocking up on *Thalia's* hand-dipped chocolates, *pastelli* and miniature *amygdalota* (crushed almond balls). Thalia has a tiny shop on the waterfront near the ticket agent.

1 *Otzia*
2 *The Lion*
3 *Koundouros*
4 *Karthaia beach*
5 *View from Kastriani*
6 *Country church*

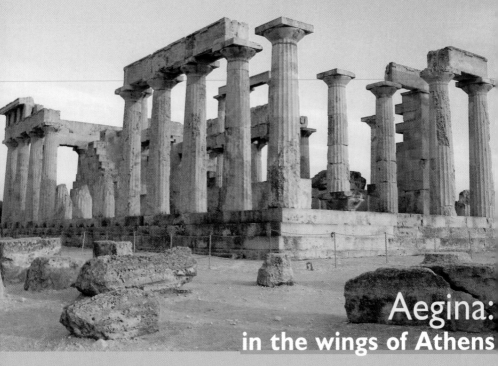

Aegina:
in the wings of Athens

Every time I visit Aigina for the day, I make the same mistake. Although I've heard the town is delightful, I never leave time enough to explore and enjoy it. Friends who know it well talk about excellent *ouzeris* around the fishmarket, original little shops on the inner streets, statues and buildings dating from the two years when Aigina was the first capital of modern Greece. Silly me, I always think we'll see these things in the hour before the boat leaves for Piraeus, but somehow we get embroiled in the mad scramble for the ferry instead.

O n a recent springlike Sunday, with more than eight hours ahead of us, I was sure there would be plenty of time to spare for a leisurely stroll around the port. We started at the beginning. In other words, we made our way north of the waterfront to the single column standing on the headland, which is all that's left of a 6th century BC temple of Apollo. Though old, this is by no means the earliest of Aigina's building projects. In fact, the site (known as 'Kolonna') was first settled in neolithic times and the tangle of rough stone walls looped below the temple foundations belongs to houses lived in five thousand years ago. Heaped on top and around them are Roman fortifications, Byzantine cisterns and masses of wild flowers, but no Classical remains whatsover.

This island paid the price for being too successful. Poised midway between Attica and the Peloponnese, Aigina became a panhellenic power before Athens, Corinth and Sparta were fledgling city-states. Stony soil meant the islanders' livelihood had to come from the sea, and by the 7th century Aigina's ships ruled the Aegean. Traders relied on its silver coins, the first such currency in Europe, with sea turtles on one side, tortoises on the other; its artists, sculptors and potters were in demand throughout Greece; and its system of weights and measures set the standard. This prosperity and, especially, its naval supremacy rankled the growing superpower across the gulf, and after the battle of Salamis, where the island's fleet shared the credit for defeating the Persians, the Athenians decided to deal with the Aiginetan threat. In 457 BC, some twenty years later, Athenian soldiers demolished her walls, shut down the mint, and forced Aigina into the League of loyal city-states. Still uneasy at the start of the Peloponnesian War, Pericles routed the islanders, who found sanctuary with the Spartans. The anti-Aigina sentiment was so intense that even Aristotle proclaimed it the "eyesore of Piraeus." Eventually the refugees did return, but the island never again made history in ancient times.

You can see remnants of its potters' and sculptors' prowess in the small museum near the entrance to the site. Grave steles line the forecourt, while inside a characteristically enigmatic sphinx guards the exhibits: Cycladic, Mycenaean, Geometric and Archaic pottery and fragments from the frieze at the Temple of Aphaia across the island. Mostly disembodied feet, legs and arms, their presence is a sad reminder that Athenians were not the only powers to plunder Aigina. In 1811 German and British archaeologists removed the pediment sculptures, which portrayed episodes in the Trojan War, and auctioned them off to Ludwig of Bavaria. They have been in Munich's Glyptothek ever since. To add insult to injury, most of the sculpture excavated later was installed in the National Museum in Athens.

Still, there is plenty of sculpture in Aigina – modern classics by Christos Kapralos, a native of Agrinio, who adopted the island in 1961. Like Attica, Aigina possesses a special light that spellbinds artists, so as you follow the signs to the Kapralos Museum a few kilometers beyond Kolonna, you pass a series of large, attractive houses overlooking inviting pebbled coves. There are few plaques to distinguish their owners, but several major 20th century talents live or lived here: Moralis, Nikolaou, architect Aris Konstantinidis, and Kazantzakis, who wrote *Zorba the Greek* during his stay. Aigina is also the home of choice of many poets and writers, Greek and foreign, and even supports a literary magazine.

Despite the open gate, the red shutters of Kapralos's house were firmly shut. We peered into studio windows and studied the marble and stone works exposed on the terraces, the bronze Mother standing like a beacon on a rock near the sea. Some sculptures show a sense of humor – delicate bronze hands reaching out from barely worked stone blocks towards a shapely marble torso, an animal's hindquarters doubling as a chair – while the best are monumental, pared down to the essential, simple yet powerful. Most of these are hewn from wood and are sheltered inside the studios, which a woman appeared from next door to open when we had all but given up hope. Christina Petropoulou was a child when

The island paid the price for being too successful.

Kapralos first came to Aigina and her proudly revealed secrets brought the master to life: "He worked hard most of the day but in the evening he drank with his friends, especially Moralis. Wine was his greatest pleasure (*to krasaki itan to meraki tou*)", she said as she pointed out the wine cellar.

Christina made sure we paid due attention to every piece before she unlocked the door to his magnum opus, a series of terra-cotta relief plaques, 40 meters long, 1.10 meters high, dedicated to the Battle of Pindos: farmers with scythes, kilted soldiers with bayonets, women dancing, people starving, and finally, everyone gathered 'round a hurdy-gurdy celebrating the end of the war – all in an extremely moving archaic style. What we saw, though, was a copy. Since autumn of last year the original can be viewed in the Parliament building in Syntagma Square.

By now, it was already well past two, time to be enjoying a fish lunch at Perdika, a kaiki harbor that

has surrendered to sleek speedboats. On the way we passed grove after grove of pistachio trees, the crop that saved Aigina from being swamped by summer houses and shabby hotels. Imported from Egypt in the late 19th century, they quickly took over most of the available land in the west of the island. These trees produce smaller nuts than their competitors in Iran and Turkey, but connoisseurs find them even more delicious.

This south side of the island, where few trees grow, has the same blood-red volcanic rocks as Methana, whose jagged bulk loomed under a cloak of mist on the horizon. As we drove up the side of Aigina's cone-shaped mountain, whose name is simply that, 'Oros', we passed molten-looking boulders that must have solidified as soon as they spewed into existence. A tiny white church dots the tip, where a shrine

Aegina:
in the wings
of Athens

to Zeus Hellanion, the Rainbearer, once stood. On a slope below it, and therefore much more accessible, a magnificent and somewhat incongruous flight of stairs rises to the terraced foundation of a long-vanished temple, since occupied by a 13th century Byzantine church.

We had tramped all over this site last year. Then we had also visited the Temple of Aphaia and explored Palaiohora, Aigina's capital from the 9th century until 1826, when pirates and Turks ceased to be a danger. The temple is one of the best preserved in Greece, with 24 of its original 32 outer columns still standing, sections of intact wall separating the inner chambers, and even a two-story colonnade in the interior. Completed in the late 6th or early 5th century BC on the same pine-wooded hilltop as two earlier temples, it was dedicated to the Cretan mother goddess, Britomartis. Pausanias says that she fled Crete to escape from Minos, who was making a nuisance of himself. She leapt into a fishing boat, but the crew also behaved like brutes, so her only recourse was to swim. There must have been safety closer than Aigina, but she wasn't taking any chances, and as soon as she set foot on the island, she disappeared into the woods, becoming invisible – *aphanis* in Greek. In time, her identity merged with that of Athena, and it is a copy of her statue that you see in the Aphaia Museum.

Built on a hillside half way between Aphaia and the port, medieval Palaiohora with its forty churches and other ruins is worth an article in itself and several hours of dipping in and out of them. Only one or two of the churches have been restored, and one wishes that a fraction of the millions lavished on the ornate rotunda dedicated to St. Nektarios just below Palaiohora could have been diverted to saving Aigina's Byzantine heritage. The first Greek Orthodox saint to be canonized in the 20th century, Nektarios was a humble, scholarly monk who founded a monastery in Aigina in the early 1900s. He lived in a small house and prayed under a pine tree. I can't help thinking he would have been appalled at the ostentatious disregard for setting embodied in this new construction, which can hold 9000 worshippers.

I like to think he would have wished some of that money was spent helping Aigina's Wild Animal Hospital, where ten permanent Greek and foreign volunteers work tirelessly and cheerfully to save thousands of injured birds every year. Last year the hospital moved from the port to more spacious quarters near the shrine with the staircase. The land was donated by the Chryssoleontissa Monastery above it, the buildings and aviaries by the Nomarchia of Piraeus, but no provision was made for operating expenses, which have to be covered by donations.

Maria Ghika showed us around, but not too close to the aviaries, where hundreds of birds, most of

them recuperating from wounds inflicted by trigger-happy hunters, were awaiting eventual liberation. Owls, hawks, swans, eagles, storks, flamingos, waders of all sorts, all had their own large cages, but what astonished us most of all were the vultures. There were twenty-five in the aviary, another six or seven hunkering over it! A similar population of free waterfowl was crowded around the cage with their injured compatriots, making the hospital one of the most populated wildlife refuges in this country. Birds of a feather certainly live up to their reputation.

As we said goodbye to Maria and gave a final tickle to Miko, a raccoon rescued from a Czech fur farm by Cephalonians who fed him chocolates, the sun was low on the horizon. We barely had time to get in line for the ferry, let alone to explore the port's back streets and Capodistrian monuments. Foiled again, I would just have to come back for more. ○

Aegina:
in the wings
of Athens

How to get there

There are probably more boats leaving Piraeus for Aigina than buses for Athens. The trip can vary between 1/2 hour and almost 2, depending on whether you catch a hydrofoil, a modern ferry or the old-fashioned, heel-less slipper variety (nicknamed *pantofla* by Greeks). Call 210 4117341, 4171190, or 4199983-4 for schedules and bookings. If you're on a tight schedule, book your return at the same time, because boats fill up quickly at peak times, on Sunday nights especially. If you don't take your own car, you can rent a car or motorbike on the waterfront opposite the ferry landing.

Where to eat

In the port, friends who live in Aigina divide their time between *O Vangelis* (also called Lekkas) and *O Batis*, near the ferry dock, *O Skotadis* in the middle of the waterfront, and the *ouzeris* around the fish market. In Perdika, we had superb grilled octopus and fresh fish at *Miltos Trimas's* taverna in the middle of the row of seemingly identical places overlooking the water, and there is another simple but excellent taverna at Portes, just before you turn down to the sea. The best pistachios are those produced by the Aigina Cooperative.

Where to stay

There are dozens of hotels scattered around the island, but the port has several old houses that have been converted into charming hotels. Try *Eginitiko Archontiko* near the square with the mock medieval tower (tel. 22970 24968), or *Hotel Brown* on the water-front near the southern outskirts of town (tel. 22970 22271).

To become a member of the Hellenic Wildlife Hospital, annual subscription €25, contact their offices in Athens at 210 9520117 or in Thessaloniki at 2310 724969.

The Kapralos Museum is open Friday-Sunday from 10 am to 2 pm, the Archaeological Museum is open Tuesday-Sunday, 8:30 am-3:45 pm, and the Temple and Museum at Aphaia daily from 8:15 am to 5 pm.

1 *Temple of Aphaia*
2 *Church at Palaiohora*
3 *Mock medieval tower*
4 *Kolonna*
5 *Miko the raccoon and Maria Ghika*
6 *A hawk being packaged for delivery to its original home.*

B I B L I O G R A P H Y

Anna Alavanou, *Brauron* (Keramos Guides, Lycabettus Press, Athens, 1972).

T. Anastassiou, *Kea* (Syros, 2001).

Robin Barber, *A Guide to Rural Attika* (1999).

Robin Barber, *Blue Guide Greece* (A. & C. Black, London, 1995).

J. Theodore Bent, *The Cyclades: or Life Among the Insular Greeks* (Macmillan, London, 1884).

Char. Bouras, A. Kaloyeropoulou, R. Andreadi, *Churches of Attica* (Academy of Athens Prize, Athens, 1970).

John Caskey & E.T. Blackburn, *Lerna in the Argolid* (American School of Classical Studies, Athens, 1997).

Robert Flaceliere, *Daily Life in Greece in the time of Pericles* (Phoenix, London, 2002).

John Freely, *Strolling Through Athens* (Penguin, London, 1991).

Eridanos, the River of Ancient Athens (Hellenic Ministry of Culture, Direction of Prehistoric and Classical Antiquities, Department of Educational Programmes, Athens, 2000).

Adonis K. Kyrou, *Sto Stavrodromi tou Argolikou* (Athens, 1990).

Osbert Lancaster, *Classical Landscape with Figures* (John Murray, London, 1975).

Patrick Leigh Fermor, *Roumeli* (Penguin, London, 1987).

Liza Micheli, *Unknown Athens* (Dromena, Athens, 1990).

Stephen Miller, *The Ancient Stadium of Nemea* (no publisher or date).

Pausanias, *Guide to Greece*, volumes 1 & 2, Central Greece and Southern Greece, trans. Peter Levi, S.J. (Penguin, London, 1971).

Stephanos Psimenos, *Anexerevniti Peloponnisos* (Road Editions, Athens, 1998).

Titos P. Yiohalas, *Andros, Arvanites kai Arvanitika* (Patakis, Athens, 2000).

PHOTO CREDITS

All the photographs in this book
are by the author with the exception
of those by Petros Ladas on pages 6,
82-85, 100-108, 110, 111, 114,
122-127, 162-169, 178-191, 194-203;
Frosso Vassiliades on pages 92, 93,
216, 219, 226; and John & Annie
Apgar on pages 173, 174 (r) and 175.

Edited by Annie Correal
Design by Poppy Alexiou & Alexandra Drossou
Printed and bound in Athens by Iris S.A.

Acrocorinth